"HEAL THYSELF"

"HEAL THYSELF"

Managing Health Care Reform

Pat Armstrong
Hugh Armstrong
Ivy Lynn Bourgeault
Jacqueline Choiniere
Eric Mykhalovskiy
Jerry P. White

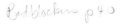

Garamond Press

Printed and bound in Canada

Garamond Press Ltd.
63 Mahogany Court
Aurora, Ontario
L4G 6M8

Canadian Cataloguing in Publication Data

Main entry under title:

Heal thyself: managing health care reform

(Health care in Canada)
Includes index.
ISBN 1-55193-024-2

1. Health care reform - Canada.   I. Armstrong,
Pat, 1945-   II. Series: Health Care in Canada
(Aurora, Ont.)

RA395.C3H417 2000   362.1'0971   C00-931047-9

*The Press acknowledges the financial assistance received
from the Government of Canada through the Book Publishing Industry
Development Program for our publishing activities.*

Contents

EBP

Acknowledgements

The two initial chapters in this book are a revised version of a paper originally commissioned by the National Co-ordinating Group on Women and Health Care Reform, a group that crosses the Centres of Excellence for Women's Health and funded by the Women's Bureau at Health Canada. While we owe a great debt to the group and to Health Canada, neither can be held responsible for the current content.

The subsequent chapters reflect the generous support of the British Columbia Nurses' Association and the Canadian Federation of Nurses' Union. Both contributed in time, money and in organizing interviews. The real heroines of this piece are the members of those unions - the women providing the care - who took the time from their overwhelming schedules to share their experiences with us and to comment on our analysis of their work. We have tried to capture their passion, concern and commitment not only for their patients but also for the public health system.

A new member in our research group, Suzanne Peters, quietly, efficiently, and effectively produced the bibliography. Carleton University and the University of Western Ontario provided financial support. Donna Dawson did a sensitive job of copy-editing. And, as always, Peter Saunders of Garamond Press has been there for us.

We dedicate this book to Kathleen Connors, President of the Canadian Federation of Nurses' Unions, who dedicates her life to care.

Introduction

Global Reform

This is a book primarily about health care reform in Canada, and the consequences of these reforms, particularly as they are assessed by registered nurses. However, health reform is a central item on the agenda of countries throughout the western world. New drugs and technologies, new research on methodologies, new teaching practices and new ways of organizing and delivering services have been introduced continually throughout the twentieth century. This is particularly the case for the period since the Second World War. Health reform, then, is not a new phenomenon. Current reforms, however, are so fundamental in scope that they constitute a qualitative change, even a revolutionary one, in health care provision.

In the immediate postwar period, health reform was concerned primarily with access–with ensuring that people received necessary care. Western countries launched a variety of public programs designed to make health care services widely available. Expenditures on health services grew rapidly, along with improvements in both access to and the quality of care. Although health care in many countries continued to be provided, or paid for, by governments, more and more profits were made in this sector as well. In recent years, the major focus of reform has been on cost containment, on controlling how much is spent, especially by governments and by employers. Quality and governance have also been central concerns, and there is much more discussion of health promotion, although even these issues have been viewed through the lens of expenditure reduction.

To some extent, this transformation in health care reform is evident throughout the western world. A comparative analysis of reform in seven of these countries identifies "unacceptably rapid increases in health expenditures" as a central problem, along with "inefficiency and poor performance" and "remaining gaps in access to services."[1] According to this study from the Organization for Economic Co-operation and Development (OECD), the problems in health care are the result of two different kinds of circumstances.

The first is "demographic and technological change." The increasing preponderance of elderly people in the population and the increasing use of expensive equipment and methods for care are defined as "mainly or partly outside the control of governments."[2]

The second circumstance is "remediable flaws in the way in which the financing, payment and regulation systems for health care are designed." That these circumstances are defined as "remediable flaws" reflects the position that they can be corrected primarily through better management.[3] And increasingly, better management is defined as practices taken from the private, for-profit sector and applied to the provision of care. As another OECD publication puts it, "Most strategies for health reform are based on the principles of market-based resources allocation."[4]

It is thus the preoccupation with rising expenditures that has provided the primary justification for the conversion to market-based strategies in health care, although it provides only part of the motivation. For those promoting these approaches, the assumptions are clear: price competition in the market, combined with consumer choice, produces the most efficient and effective management techniques. Such techniques simultaneously reduce costs while ensuring quality. Not incidently, they also open space for profit-making in care. Although many of these managerial strategies were designed for the production of goods, their proponents assume that they are equally applicable to the provision of care.

To control prices and in some cases increase profits, market-based techniques seek to change where, how and on what basis decisions about appropriate and necessary care are made. These new managerial strategies involve more than transforming the way care is financed. They also involve a significant shift in power away from providers and patients, placing managers or owners in charge.

In Canada, the federal and provincial governments have made reform of the health care system a top priority in recent years. As is the case with other countries, cost control has been a central concern and arguably the driving force behind reform strategies in Canada's mainly non-profit system. Certainly a range of issues has been considered by the various commissions charged with making recommendations on health reform. But financial pressures have played the major role, as have pressure from firms seeking to make money in health care. Response to both kinds of pressure has meant the route to expenditure control is defined mainly as a management matter. Recommendations on human resources and organization "overlap with those suggested for financial and managerial issues," as Douglas Angus points out in his review of major commissions.[5] The commissions have shared a conviction that new managerial strategies are, in the words of the 1991 *Report* from the British Columbia Royal Commission on Health Care and Costs, "a key to effective and efficient delivery of health services."[6] And many of these managerial strategies are ones taken or adapted from the for-profit sector in the United States.

There has been, then, a lot of talk in Canada about reforming care to save care. It is talk that is difficult to assess in isolation from other developments in global forces. To understand the dramatic changes under way in Canadian health care, it is necessary to understand the pressures and ideas that are dominant both here and abroad.

Chapter 1 describes the context for health reform, a context that sets the stage for local initiatives. It outlines the development of welfare states in the period following the Second World War, and explains how we established a publicly funded health care system in Canada. Chapter 2 examines more recent changes in Canada that have fundamentally challenged the welfare state and the health care services it provides.

The Model For Health Care Reform

The model for current reforms is the private for-profit sector. A variety of claims have been made about the benefits of this model, claims that relate to both quality of care and cost. Yet there are at least three major differences between health care delivery and goods production; these differences raise significant questions about how appropriate market-based techniques are for the provision of health care.

First, care providers assume and demand autonomy in making decisions based on their assessment of individual need. This is particularly the case with doctors, who determine many health care expenditures. In contrast, strategies in the for-profit sector assume and demand managerial control over processes and decision-making. It is not surprising, then, that the regulation of providers is central to these new approaches and a matter of great dispute in health care reform.

A second major difference between the two sectors relates to sales. In the for-profit sector, selling more is critical to maintaining profit growth. Customers are encouraged to spend and use more. In health care reform, however, the stated purpose is to spend and use less. Utilization reviews are intended to reduce the number of procedures performed and processes used as a means of both lowering costs and improving care. These reviews, however, have also been a source of contention because they limit both access to services and providers' capacity to make decisions on the basis of their assessments of individual need.

This, in turn, is related to another major difference between health care delivery and for-profit production. Customer choice is defined as a primary basis for competition in the market. But, as the OECD points out, health care is "often highly unpredictable."[7] As a result, many patients lack the knowledge, the capacity or the time to decide among alternatives. In other words, many are not in a position to exercise the choice that is seen as a fundamental basis for efficiency in for-profit firms. This unpredictability makes care delivery less amenable to managerial planning and costing based on assumptions about regularity and uniformity among products.

Although the for-profit sector has become a model for much of health care management, there has been little research demonstrating that the management practices developed mainly with profits and goods production in mind will be either effective or efficient in the delivery of care in Canada's largely non-profit care system. The adoption of the for-profit model has been based more on faith than on evidence, in spite of a discourse that stresses evidence.

The research analysed in chapters 3, 4 and 5 is designed as an initial step in assessing these new ways of managing health care. In particular, the research focuses on the following major claims made by health care management in both the for-profit and non-profit sectors:

1. **Integrated systems** ensure **continuity of care** from service to service. Integration involves the consolidation and merging of resources throughout the system.[8] There are two basic forms of integration. By coordinating patient care services "across people, facilities, functions, activities and time,"[9] new managerial strategies seek to reduce duplication and gaps in the system. By requiring access through a general practitioner, new managerial strategies seek to regulate unnecessary use while providing continuity and integrated care in a manner that eliminates fragmentation. "The ultimate goals are to benefit the consumer (patient) by improving the overall quality and

continuity of services provided and to benefit the taxpayer by making the system more efficient and cost effective."[10]

2. Making providers and patients **accountable** ensures that **appropriate care** is delivered to the people who need it. With utilization review, standardization through measurement and work reorganization, new managerial strategies seek to improve the **quality of care** "through concerted attention to care processes."[11] "Quality evaluation would include accurate needs assessments, indicators of quality improvement initiatives, economic evaluation, measurement of self-reported health status and monitoring of member and provider satisfaction."[12]

3. An emphasis on **health promotion and disease and injury prevention** ensures that people stay healthy, that reform moves "from managing care to managing health." New managerial strategies seek to both reduce costs and improve health through this emphasis on health promotion and sickness prevention. A "commitment to wellness"[13] involves a shift away from the "focus on the treatment and cure of disease"[14] that has characterized the health system in Canada over the past three decades.

These claims are assessed here through the experiences of the registered nurses who deliver care in the system undergoing reform. Our reasons for asking these nurses about the reforms are quite simple. Registered nurses make up the bulk of the health care labour force. In 1997, there were more than 200,000 registered nurses employed in Canada and three quarters of them provided direct care in institutional settings.[15] They not only experience the impact of reforms directly in their daily work, they are also often in a better position than doctors, policy makers or managers to see and assess the impact on the patients in their care. RNs have more regular and prolonged contact with patients and their families than do the physicians who direct the care or the managers who supervise the system. As a result, they are in a position to provide valuable assessments of management claims.

Our interviews with these nurses all involved group discussions with women who volunteered for the project. In this way, we could both encourage a dialogue and explore differences in views. Nurses were asked about their experiences in relation to the three claims set out above; that is, integration and continuity, accountability and quality, and health promotion and disease prevention. Both positive and negative responses were solicited in discussions that were only partially structured. Our analysis of these interviews is organized around the three kinds of claims, although the issues often overlapped.[16]

The nurses interviewed for this study all work in British Columbia, the province with the greatest increase in the total number of RNs employed between 1992 and 1997 (an 8.5 per cent increase, compared to a 1.8 per cent decrease for Canada as a whole), in headcount if not in full-time equivalent terms.[17] They work in a range of facilities and for a range of organizations. They hold a variety of views on unions and politics, and differ significantly in terms of their involvement in health reform plans. Nevertheless, their experiences with, and perspectives on, health reform are remarkably similar, and we are convinced that their experiences provide important lessons not only for reform in Canada but also for any country contemplating similar reforms.

Chapter 1

The International Context For Health Care Reform[18]

Health reform has seldom been a strictly local matter. North America's first hospital was established in what is now Quebec City early in the seventeenth century by three Augustinian nuns, funded by a French noblewoman.[19] Their devotion helped establish the notion of caring in nursing. Women in uniforms still provide most of the formal health care services today, based in many ways on the principles set out by Florence Nightingale, the British "lady with the lamp." In 1910, the Carnegie Foundation commissioned a US educator, Abraham Flexner, to examine medical training across North America. His resulting report had a profound impact not only on how doctors are educated and licensed but also on how health care services are delivered.[20] It marked the firm entrenchment of science and the medical model, an emphasis still quite visible today. When Sir William Beveridge drew up his plan for social insurance in Britain during the Second World War, he provided what Malcolm Taylor described as "a ready-made base" for Canadian health insurance, "although many of its recommendations would have to be fundamentally altered for application in a federal state."[21]

Canada has developed some unique reform strategies and adapted others to suit our particular circumstances. And we have not been without influence abroad. This is particularly the case in the areas of health promotion[22] and gender-based analysis. But foreign influences and external pressures have seldom been absent, although the extent and nature of these have changed significantly over the years. Health reform, then, has to be understood within an international context.

This chapter seeks to locate current reforms, outlining some of the pressures and influences that are shaping strategies to change health care in Canada. It begins by setting out the philosophy and conditions at the international and then at the national level that led to the development of Canada's public health care system. It then moves on to outline the new paradigm dominant in the international and national arena.

The Aftermath of War

The International Stage

The Second World War set the stage for radical health care reform. The Great Depression had demonstrated that unfettered markets could not ensure the appropriate production and delivery of either goods or services. It had also demonstrated that Canadians, when facing so much deprivation, were prepared to take direct action against governments. The war marked the end, for a while at least, of not only the protests and the deprivation, but also of small government and, along with it, of the notion that the invisible hand of the market would provide.

Most countries involved in the war emerged from it with large state sectors, huge debts and populations that demanded better conditions in return for the sacrifices they had made for the war effort. As Malcolm Taylor put it,

> There was a mood of rebellion against the universal risks of unemployment and sickness, disability and old age, widowhood and poverty, a pervasive dissatisfaction with precarious minimum wages, drought-stricken farms, grudgingly-granted relief payments, and a suspiciously-administered, means-tested old age pension.[23]

Women were very much part of this rebellion. "CCF women, for example, demanded leadership training programs, publicly accessible birth control clinics and equal pay laws as early as the mid-1930s."[24] Indeed, the federal government was so concerned about what women would do after the war that it set up a special task force to report on the *Post-War Problems of Women*.[25] Unions too were active in demanding greater public intervention, as were professional organizations representing doctors and nurses.

Although Allied governments feared massive revolt and a return to high unemployment in the aftermath of war, they were not driven simply by these fears. There was an optimism about state intervention, based on Keynesian economics and the experiences of the war years. There was also a new view of cooperation among countries. For centuries, the increasingly global economy had prompted calls for some kind of international regulation. But it took the Second World War to convince decision-makers "that industrial countries, in particular, were too advanced, specialized, and interdependent to contemplate genuine, lasting improvements in economic welfare after the war without re-establishing some sort of new economic order."[26] Equally important, they saw the task as "too important and urgent for the postwar recovery to be left to the slow, haphazard processes of the markets, whose limitations had been exposed in the interwar period."[27] Among the various women's movements, there was "great hope not just for women's advancement but also for social improvement via active good government."[28] Similarly, professional organizations and unions saw important benefits in a social wage.

There were certainly disagreements, and opponents to these developments. However, at least according to one analyst of the period, "the powerful vested interests that might have resisted this successfully were too shell-shocked and marginalized by the disastrous turn of events in the 1930s and early 1940s to put up much of a resistance."[29] At the same time, there were multiple opportunities for investment and profit-making available in the wake of the war's destruction, as well as the development of new technologies and generous government infrastructure support for business. And in the aftermath of war austerity, there was considerable pent-up consumer demand. There was, therefore, limited incentive for businesses to resist the expansion, or at least maintenance, of state intervention and international regulations.

A variety of organizations resulted from the Bretton Woods agreements of 1946–47 and the establishment of the United Nations. The World Bank and the International Monetary Fund (IMF), officially specialized agencies of the United Nations, were intended to coordinate the international financial system. The World Health Organization (WHO), the United Nations Children's Emergency Fund (UNICEF), the United Nations Development Fund (UNDP) and the United Nations Fund for Population Activities (UNFPA) were designed to develop a range of health strategies throughout the world. As the constitution of the World Health Organization made clear, there was a shared understanding that the "health of all peoples is fundamental to the attainment of peace and security, and is dependent upon the fullest cooperation of individuals and states."

In keeping with the philosophy that guided the postwar years, the WHO constitution set out a central role for states in establishing the conditions and services necessary for healthy populations and for health care services. The final clause is unequivocal: "Governments have a responsibility for the health of their people which can be fulfilled only by the provision of adequate health and social measures."[30] At the same time, the technologies and therapies developed during the war contributed to a growing faith in, and demand for, health care services. Not surprisingly, then, most industrialized countries developed or expanded public health care services during this period, placing a particular emphasis in North America on the most expensive services–hospital and medical care. By 1995, in 20 of the 29 countries surveyed by the OECD, "more than 70 per cent of total expenditure on health takes place in the public sector" and in seven of these countries, the public share was more than 80 per cent.[31] A significant sector of the labour involved in care was commodified, with a growing number of women paid to do the care work, while men continued to dominate major decision-making. Although critiques of the medical model were not absent, the primary issues were framed in terms of access to existing health care services that were assumed to provide quality care.

There was, in these health discussions, a recognition of different health needs for women, although women were not central participants in the international agreements or in the organizations they set up. At least one obvious women's issue was given priority; namely, maternal and child health.[32] This reflected the tendency to define women's health needs in terms of their reproductive capacities, and to address the issue more in terms of controlling women than of empowering them.[33] In the dominant paradigm of the period, difference was often understood as biologically determined inferiority, and solutions were offered in terms of a western medical model.

Matters related to women as paid and unpaid providers were not central concerns in these international debates, and it is difficult to find documentation of discussions at the international meetings about the division of labour within or outside health care services. These issues were not, however, absent from debates among women, nor were women simply passively accepting the dominant paradigm. Although the consequences of the interventions varied for different groups of women, and from country to country as well as from region to region, and were often contradictory, many women benefitted from the development of initiatives in such areas as public health and public care services, nutrition and sanitation initiatives, and as patients, providers and decision-makers. Paid jobs in health care grew, and along with them, the strength of many women.[34]

Indeed, inequality in general declined with more services provided by the state and with more regulation of the private sector. Benefits were not equally distributed, but more attention was paid to those with disabilities and more support was provided as well.

Canadian Initiatives

It was in this context that Canada reformed postwar health care services. At the national political level, the climate supported public intervention in delivery, regulation, planning and support. There was a strong federal state, buttressed by a Keynesian philosophy and by experience that supported state intervention. There were new technology- and hospital-based services that demonstrated the benefits of effective treatments and cures.

There was also a restless population demanding access to the health services that had become increasingly inaccessible in the prewar years and increasingly expensive in the postwar ones.

And as employment expanded there was a labour movement growing in strength and numbers, a movement committed to a social wage that included health care. Various women's organizations were also part of the increasing pressure for public care, as women struggled to defend not only their own interests in terms of access to care, but those of their families as well.

At the same time, there was a relative absence of for-profit services and even of insurance companies involved in health care. Nine out of ten hospitals were non-profit in 1955.[35] A significant proportion of insurance companies were also non-profit, with Blue Cross leading the pack. Large companies faced increasingly strong labour groups demanding health benefits and a public plan promised to reduce direct costs to these companies. As a result, the corporate sector offered only limited opposition to state involvement.

There was strong evidence of the need both for more services and for public care. Significant proportions of the population had no insurance coverage, and the uninsured stayed in hospitals longer than the insured, primarily because they sought care only when they were very ill. Given the high cost of care, the government often ended up paying for the care of the uninsured. Research on insurance indicated that even those with coverage had only part of their bill paid by the insuring company, and this was the case particularly if the coverage was provided by a for-profit firm. At the same time, an investigation of hospital costs found that voluntary insurance schemes were part of the problem.[36] According to the *Taylor Report*, insurance schemes added significantly to hospital expenditures: "eighteen percent in the case of Blue Cross, thirty percent in commercial group contracts, seventy percent in commercial individual contracts, and sixteen percent in the case of cooperatives."[37]

These various pressures combined to set the stage for a public health care plan. Health care was defined more as a social good than as a market commodity. The discourse was about shared risks[38] and "public responsibility for individual economic security and welfare."[39]

There was, of course, controversy and compromise. The first postwar federal/provincial conference on health care failed to reach agreement. Foiled at the conference table, the federal government used its spending power first to fund research, training and hospital construction. Then it promised to pay half the cost of hospital insurance and later, medical insurance. And finally, the 1984 *Canada Health Act* brought hospital and medical insurance together, forbidding user fees and opening the door to care outside hospitals and doctors' offices. The provinces were far from universally supportive at any stage of these developments. John Robarts, the Conservative premier of Ontario went so far as to claim at one point that the new "Machiavellian scheme" was "one of the greatest frauds that has ever been perpetrated on the people of this country."[40]

Such opposition encouraged the development of a plan based on principles set out at the federal level rather than on a detailed plan that each province would follow. In the end, the *Canada Health Act* is only thirteen pages long, and that includes text in both official languages. As a result, there is not one system but many systems, each with the possibility of adapting to local needs. The provinces and territories have used their spending power to shape regional, municipal and organizational developments, but significant choices remained at each level.

Opposition from various quarters also encouraged the development of a plan based on an insurance model rather than a provider model. The government responded to the concerns of provider organizations by leaving services in their hands. Under this model, "private insurance is implicitly or explicitly forbidden and there is no opting out of paying taxes for the public system."[41] Although the insurance plan must be publicly administered, there is no requirement in the *Canada Health Act* that the services be provided by a non-profit firm.

From the beginning, then, Canada had what would now be called a purchaser/provider split. Health care services remained for the most part in the hands of the non-profit organizations that had been providing the care, resulting in what Josephine Rekart calls public funds for private provision.[42] Under the *Canada Health Act*, these public funds went mainly to non-profit hospitals, so private meant non-profit. And non-profit organizations were often more open to public scrutiny and control. At the very least, they did not spend the care dollar on profit. However, provinces/territories and municipalities have put public funds into other forms of services, such as long-term care facilities and home care, that can be provided by for-profit firms in many jurisdictions. Some of these services were also provided under the *Canada Assistance Plan*, where the principles of the *Canada Health Act* do not apply.[43]

Opposition from a variety of sources, including insurance companies and other increasingly strong vested interests, also helped limit the scope of reform. The Hall Commission, a royal commission set up to make recommendations on medical services, originally recommended coverage of medical services, dental services, prescription drugs, optical services, prosthetic devices and home care. The purpose was to make the services not only comprehensive but appropriate. However, the plans were scaled down to cover only hospitals and doctors.[44] One result was the expansion of for-profit care in the other areas, albeit with considerable public funding.

James Struthers argues that in Ontario, for example, the combination of the federal government's offer to fund 50 per cent of the cost of both hospital care and long-term care for "unemployed indigents" provided a stimulus for the business of care,[45] often by operators with "no previous experience and few qualifications applying for licence."[46] This, in turn, led the operators to demand that the government intervene to prevent unfair competition from unscrupulous businesses. Matthew Dymond, the health minister of the time (1959) warned the Ontario premier that "The patients are overcrowded, inadequately and improperly cared for, by staffs that obviously have little or no training to equip them for the job."[47] But, according to the same health minister, the subsequent regulation, combined with public funding, did not work to protect patients or taxpayers. Instead, the nursing home operators formed a strong lobby demanding more funds. This Conservative health minister reported in 1967 that "they are concerned about one thing only, making as much money as possible and giving as little as possible in return to the patients." In the face of this evidence, he recommended that care be provided on a public basis.[48] There were regular warnings against leaving long-term care in for-profit hands and outside the public system. Ontario's solution to the problem created by for-profit care was to introduce insurance coverage for medical services provided in extended-care organizations, but not to restrict for-profit services. One consequence of this strategy, according to Struthers, is that by the end of the 1980s, 86 per cent of nursing home beds in Ontario were owned by highly profitable corporate chains, and paid for mainly with tax dollars.[49]

Another result of public health insurance was the expansion of choice, especially given the additional criteria of universality, accessibility and comprehensiveness. Because governments funded services rather than individuals, and did not provide services directly, there was a range of options available. Patients could choose among service providers and seek consultations from more than one kind of provider. Coverage was thus portable from service to service and job to job, and alterative means of delivering care were available in many areas. This was particularly important to women because they often encountered providers who dismissed their symptoms or responded in ways that reflected stereotypes and cultural values that were inappropriate to an individual woman's needs. Moreover, women are more likely to have short-term employment and thus portability from job to job is critical to ensure continuity of care.

The controversy and opposition not only reduced the scope of public care, it also shaped the nature of reform. The prolonged doctors' strike in Saskatch-ewan when provincial medical insurance was first introduced caused the government to give up its plan to introduce salaries for the medical profession. No other government has seriously taken up such a strategy since. Pressure from doctors also contributed to the limited development of the community clinics that were central to several provincial plans. This was particularly the case in Québec, where the commission charged with investigating health services envisioned a care system based on a holistic and collective model. In a series of recommendations that sounds remarkably current, the Castonguay-Nepveau Commission proposed the integration of prevention and cure through clinics designed to provide continuous rather than episodic care. In local community service centres (CLSCs), teams that included not only a range of health care providers but also those equipped to deal with economic and social issues, would work together to care for entire households within the context of their social, economic, cultural and physical locations. Everyone employed in the centres would be salaried, a strategy intended to counter the medical model and stress health promotion, broadly defined. Employees and citizens would have a say in how the centres were organized, staffed and operated. To ensure equity, continuity and financial responsibility, services were still to be centrally coordinated and the provincial government was still to have a major planning role. The vision was never realized, however, in spite of the appointment of one commissioner to the position of health minister. Resistance from doctors in particular, combined with a failure on the part of the government to follow through on the more radical parts of the plan in the face of opposition from a variety of quarters, meant that the recommen-dations were never fully implemented. The "most profitable sectors of medical care were left in private hands, while the state, through public establishments and the CLSCs took charge of the unprofitable parts: health care for the disadvantaged, and in isolated regions, preventative medicine and public health services."[50]

As was the case in other provinces, public funding served to reinforce the medical model, put more power in the hands of doctors and increase dependency on hospital- and doctor-centred treatment of body parts.[51] It was what David Naylor described as public payment for private practice.[52] Doctors were private practitioners but not mainly profit-making operations, at least not in terms of the areas covered by public health insurance. The organizations that represented their interests negotiated with governments to determine their wages. Paid on a piece-work basis, they had some control over their income but were forbidden to charge beyond fixed rates for their services. Their scope of practice was largely determined by colleges controlled by the doctors themselves. However, as the doctors argued when they opposed the introduction of medicare, there was potential for governments to transform these relations and treat doctors more as employees than as self-employed professionals.

Medicare also led to an enormous expansion of access to services. Access improved for those most in need,[53] and the majority of these were women. At the same time, the number of jobs for women grew dramatically. Between 1951 and 1961, the number of women in the health services labour force increased from 107,063 to 205,284.[54] By 1991, more than a million women were working in health and social services, representing 16 per cent of the entire female labour force.[55] This expansion in the broader public sector contributed to the development of strong professional and union organizations among women, organizations that have fought successfully for better conditions and relations at work and for the recognition and defence of the skilled nature of their labour.[56]

A women's health movement also emerged. Women have long been active in public and occupational health, in demanding access to services, in offering health education and in promoting self-regulation, as well as better conditions, for paid care providers. In other words, they stressed what today would be called the determinants of health and health promotion, albeit often framed by wealthy women for the poorer classes. By contrast, much of the initial focus of the postwar movement was on a critique of medicine, in terms of the emphasis on a medical model, on medical power and on institutional care. Self-help, empowerment through shared knowledge and alternative therapies were central strategies in the movement that began in the 1960s.[57] It expanded to challenge the entire paradigm dominant in health services and the assumptions made not only about women's bodies and women's relations, but also about their work.

Although there is no single, unified women's health movement, empowerment, community, self-help, alternative therapies, disease prevention and health promotion, and rights have all been central to the discourse around the movement. The movement began to stress both sameness and difference,[58] both women as people who take action and women as a group that has few choices to make. The emphasis has been increasingly on connections rather than on isolated individuals; on emotions as well as on reason; on needs as well as on wants; on multiple, rather than on single, strategies; and on the concrete along with the abstract or general.[59] For most people involved in the movement, analysis begins with the socially and materially located whole person. As Susan Sherwin puts it in her introduction to *The Politics of Women's Health*, it is necessary "to address ways in which oppression may contribute to the range of choices available and may affect the weight an oppressed person must assign each option."[60] Context matters. So do relations with others. These relations, and locations, are understood to have a profound impact on health in general, and on choice in particular.

Of course, women were not alone in developing such critiques or in making such demands. However, because women comprise the majority of patients and providers, and because they suffered from patriarchal practices, women's movements were particularly active on health issues.

Summary of the Postwar Context

The postwar period was dominated by a paradigm that promoted state intervention in planning, in funding, in regulating and legislating, and even in the direct provision of some goods and services. In health care, governments began mainly by funding existing services, educational institutions and research, but moved on to intervene more directly in terms of where services where located, who provided care under what conditions and how research was conducted. Health care was defined as a public good, a shared risk and a shared responsibility. And the research on the impact of postwar strategies demonstrated that public financing "is a powerful cost control mechanism"[61] and a means of improving access, especially for the least advantaged groups.

Although services were delivered mainly by non-governmental agencies and individuals in Canada, hospitals were almost entirely non-profit organizations and doctors were paid fees negotiated with the government for most of their services. Virtually all services provided within the hospitals and all necessary doctor care were paid for from the public purse, without user fees. Outside hospitals and doctors' offices, and thus usually outside the umbrella of the *Canada Health Act,* the scene was much more varied. A mixture of small for-profit and not-for-profit organizations initially provided the services, often with significant support from government. Costs and care work increasingly became public responsibilities, although the delivery of services was in private and semi-private hands.

Women in particular benefited from the public system, in terms of both access and employment. So did other marginalized groups. These features in turn expanded their choices and helped shift some aspects of power. At the same time, the public funding of the existing system reinforced and expanded old practices that perpetuated not only women's subordination but also other inequalities and a medical model of care.[62]

After the Welfare State

There has been a decided shift within public policy and administration away from a concern with "market failure" and towards the notion of "government failure". Up to the mid-1970s, attention was focused upon why "free" markets often produce negative effects on society and economy. Now the attention is more upon the perceived deficiencies of government intervention.[63]

The Emerging Paradigm

For 25 years after the Second World War, what has been described as the postwar consensus largely held.[64] But by the early 1970s, the international agreements that reflected a Keynesian approach had begun to unravel. Both the US withdrawal from the gold standard and the increases in petroleum prices marked a major turning point in philosophy and practices at the international and national levels. While there is disagreement over the cause of this change, there is little dispute that a new philosophy guided international development.[65]

In contrast to the Keynesian approach, the new neoliberal paradigm placed its faith in a "free economy and a strong state."[66] The theory certainly called for a dismantling of the welfare state, but not for a weak state in such areas as control of the money supply or moral authority. As Brendan Martin points out in his analysis of public sector reform, it "is not *whether* or not the state intervenes in the economy that has changed but *how*, and to whose benefit."[67] The emphasis on free markets required positive intervention by the state to maintain the conditions for the free market and for social order. This means deregulating much of economic activity and regulating more of labour and personal activities. British prime minister Margaret Thatcher, for example, argued that social decay required strong government to support a return to principled morality.[68] "Special interests," such as women's groups and unions, were often seen as part of this decay.[69]

At the same time, the belief in market mechanisms supported the move to privatize public corporations to contract out services in the public sphere and to apply for-profit principles to the public sector. The assumption is made that the for-profit sector is necessarily efficient and effective, in contrast to public sector organizations, which are assumed to be bloated, bureaucratic and ineffective. As economist Paul Starr put it,

> Indeed, some supporters tout privatization as a sovereign cure for virtually all ailments of the body politic. They prescribe it as a tonic for efficiency and economic growth, an appetite suppressant for the federal budget, a vaccine against bureaucratic empire-building, and a booster for individual freedom, including the opportunities of disadvantaged minorities.[70]

In this paradigm, the market is seen "as a provider of economic efficiency and as a guarantor of a sense of individual freedom and responsibility."[71] Each firm and each individual, by pursuing its own interests would stimulate the economy, eliminate waste and expand choice. Unlike Keynesian theory, which assumed shared risks and the right to collectively provided supports, the neoliberal approach focused on freedom from economic interference. Equity was the result of each person facing the same market conditions. The benefits would supposedly trickle down to the disadvantaged, providing far better results than universal programs that were defined as encouraging dependency and stifling choice.[72] The result would be a happy marriage of efficiency, effectiveness and equity. "However, a growing body of evidence indicates that this assumption does not hold."[73] Large numbers of women throughout the world have seen their conditions deteriorate, while only a minority have experienced the trickle-down effect.[74] Inequality in general has increased, both within and among countries.

The new emphasis on the private sector coincided with failures in, and critiques of, the public sector. The OECD, for example, lists as factors leading to "the reappraisal of the rationale for government intervention" both "a perception that the public sector performance was inferior to that of the private sector" and "citizens' demands for improved responsiveness, choice and quality of service."[75] The collapse of the Soviet Union, and the accompanying notion that state expansion was a central cause, helped fuel this development. *Reinventing Government* became the guide to and justification for more and more governments, and to their participation at the global level. In this influential book, David Osborne and Ted Gaebler maintained that "market-oriented governments" should "steer," not "row" or "run things."[76] "And perhaps the most powerful method of steering is structuring the marketplace: creating incentives that move people in the direction the community wants to go, while letting them make most of the decisions."[77] In this new framework, citizens are increasingly described as customers "who can choose in a market-like fashion between different service providers"; community choices were defined mainly as individual consumer ones.[78]

Women's groups were among the most active critics of government services. For instance, they objected to the medicalization of daily life supported by a government-funded hospital and physician system. Although both physicians and hospitals remained outside government hands in many countries, state policies clearly played a critical role in how care was delivered and in the extent to which, and the manner in which, women participated in decision-making. Medical schools and other forms of education for health providers came under attack both for the exclusion of women and for the way women were included. Similarly, the male bias in the definitions, content, methods and models in state-supported medical research was exposed. The quality of care became a central concern as women pointed to the considerable variations in such areas as Caesarean section rates and the failure to monitor physician practices.

At the same time, policies and practices seldom took differences between women and men, or those among women, into account. The effectiveness and appropriateness of treatment became a central concern. Women were equally critical of the failure of governments to support alternative therapies and alternative ways of delivering care, as well as of the limited attention paid to the determinants of health and primary care. Lack of integration and continuity in services was also raised as an issue, along with the white, European, male health model that dominated care services in a way that served to limit access and negatively shape care for many women. Equity that involved recognition of differences, especially in terms of context, capacity and power, was a major goal; simply receiving equal treatment was not enough. Social justice was also a goal, and women's groups pointed out that it was not one that was always the result of public intervention.[79]

Although women were among the most critical of public-sector health interventions, this did not necessarily imply private-sector solutions. Susan Sherwin, for example, persuasively argued "that the institution of medicine has been designed in ways that reinforce sexism, and the effects of medical practice are often bad for women," but remained committed to "reforming rather than rejecting many (although not all) existing health care arrangements."[80] Women's groups particularly objected to the role that for-profit companies played in drugs and devices, demanding greater government control.[81] Indeed, at the same time as they attacked government interventions for their content, structure, methods and delivery of services, women's groups appealed to international and national organizations involved in governance to intervene on behalf of women and to assess the consequences of their actions for women. Such groups demonstrated that interventions had a differential, and often inappropriate, impact on women as citizens, patients, providers and decision-makers. And these groups have been successful in demanding a gender-based analysis of all such interventions.

Their success is not without contradictions, however. One such contradiction has to do with the context for gender-based analysis. Take the example of reproductive rights. Rosalind Petchesky argues that the 1994 Programme of Action of the Cairo International Conference on Population and Development "enshrines an almost feminist vision of reproductive rights and gender equality in place of the old population control discourse and retains a mainstream model of development under which that vision cannot possibly be realized."[82]

Petchesky goes on to explain that the Programme of Action represents the successful results of years of effort by women's groups around the world to "gain recognition of women's reproductive and sexual self-determination as a basic health need and human right."[83] Yet, the Programme not only failed "to address the real implications of privatization,"[84] but went so far as to make a commitment to "increase involvement of the private sector."[85] In Petchesky's words,

> the Cairo document promotes the very privatization, commodification and deregulation of reproductive health services that, by its own admission, have led to diminished access and increasing mortality and morbidity for poor women, who constitute "the most vulnerable groups" in both developing and developed countries.[86]

Another contradiction has to do with both the discourse surrounding reform and the demand for change. As Josephine Rekart makes clear, there is a great deal of overlap in the language used by a range of groups involved in reform.[87] Those seeking to dismantle the public system and those seeking to preserve it, albeit through changing forms, share a discourse around community and health promotion, continuity and integration, informed consent and self-help, accountability and empowerment, quality and effectiveness, primary care and local control, choice and equity. Yet the opponents and defenders of public health care mean quite different things by these concepts. The risk is that, in the context of a dominant paradigm that promotes market methods and delivery along with individual responsibility, it will not be women's understandings that prevail. Instead, women's language and critiques could be used to encourage support for strategies that deny their goals. Just as those involved in the reform of mental health services found their critiques used to justify deinstitutionalization, which left many patients without care and those that remained in care with often worse services,[88] so too are women's groups seeing their arguments used to justify market solutions to health service problems.[89]

The same could be said of other groups demanding reform. Although women had particular concerns that led them to critique the publicly funded system, they were part of a larger development that raised issues about health care. The groups supporting health promotion were critical of the "medical monopoly and the overemphasis on hospitalization."[90] While many of those involved in encouraging health promotion stressed the structural barriers to well-being, their arguments and evidence were often used to justify reductions in state subsidies and a stress on individual responsibility for health. Similarly, groups that demonstrated the importance of food, shelter, jobs and joy to determining health saw their research used to justify cutbacks to care that were not accompanied by state support for alternatives or for strategies that would enhance employment, income, nutrition or social support.

The Debt/Deficit Pressure
Debt and deficits emerged as a major problem during this period. Governments throughout the industrialized world were spending more than they were taking in each year, leaving them with deficits on an annual basis and debt loads over time. Undoubtedly the situation was serious, as more and more tax dollars went to pay interest on these debts.

There have been great debates about what caused these fiscal problems for the state. In the dominant theory, we need look no further for the explanation than the welfare state itself. The debt was caused by inefficient state bureaucracies,[91] as well as by what the OECD described as "demands of public sector staff."[92] Public choice analysts in particular saw bureaucrats protecting their own interests rather than protecting the public. The theory assumes that such interests inevitably lead to expansion, although the significant variation among states in terms of expansion would tend to deny this claim, and certainly the for-profit sector also has these tendencies.[93] Indeed, because the aim of the for-profit sector is growth, it is difficult to see how privatization will lead to contraction. It is the case that unionization spread in the public sector during this period. Brought together in large, public-sector workplaces, women in particular had demanded better wages and working conditions. However, they had started from very low levels indeed and wages, especially at the top, are often significantly lower in the public sector than in the for-profit one.

The dominant theory also found the explanation for the debt in overspending on social services, services that simultaneously created dependencies while undermining the incentive to work. Too many people saw the social wage as a right and benefits were too generous. Abuse was rampant, especially among lone-parent women and the users of health care, the majority of whom are women. There was not enough emphasis on responsibility and individual initiative. At the same time, regulation of the market and high taxes, combined with strong labour and high wages, acted as a disincentive to investment. Yet two economists from Statistics Canada who examined the growth in debt in Canada concluded that "Expenditures on social programs did not contribute significantly to the growth of government spending relative to the GDP."[94] Instead, the debt was largely the result of the way it was financed, of interest rates and of the reduction of taxes in some areas. Moreover, Canada has quite low payroll taxes compared to other industrialized countries and our overall tax rates compare favourably with those in the United States, suggesting that high taxes cannot explain much of the debt in industrialized countries.[95]

It is nonetheless important to note that unemployment rose throughout the industrialized world after changes in monetarist policies in the 1970s. This in turn contributed to rising social expenses. But it is debatable whether or not this rise was caused by the welfare state alone. In *Shrinking the State,* the authors argue that it was "the contradictions of monetarist fiscal policy mixed with the Keynesian welfare state system that necessarily produced the political economy of public debt."[96] Whatever the cause, the rising unemployment rates also served to limit the strength of labour demands on both governments and corporations.

Certainly health expenditures continued to grow, as they had throughout the postwar period, and these expenditures are not as directly related to unemployment. According to the OECD, it was "the pace of technological development in the health sector, and the demands of governments to constrain both total spending and the rising expectations of consumers" that were major factors leading to health care reform.[97] But the data also indicate that the most rapidly rising costs were those related to sectors dominated by for-profit management and those that involved private, rather than public, expenditures. Indeed, public health systems have been the most successful at cost control.[98] This would suggest that the problem was not exclusively to be found in welfare state expenditures. Employment, and labour costs, did rise, although not at the same rate. This money, moreover, cannot be treated simply as an expense. The mainly female labour force contributes directly to the economy by spending its earnings and paying its taxes.

The debt and new pressures to compete globally resulting from liberalized trade policies are frequently offered as other reasons to reduce public expenditure on health care. However, as economist Harold Chorney demonstrates, debt burdens were not nearly as high as they were in the immediate postwar period, when governments chose to develop the welfare state.[99] There are still choices today, as the variations in national strategies attest.[100]

The Limits to Care[101]

Another factor encouraging reform was a growing conviction about the limits of public care. This idea about limits took at least two forms. The first had to do with the notion that the demands on health care were unlimited, especially in the face of an aging population.[102] According to James Struthers, the issue is far from new. As early as 1941, Toronto hospitals started discharging elderly patients into nursing homes as a way of saving money. Politicians began talking about the "astounding increase in the number of persons living beyond 65 years of age," describing this aging as "the greatest social problem of our day."[103] The same language is being used four decades later to talk about the need for restraint.[104] Yet Henry Aaron points out in his presentation to the OECD that "the aging of populations cannot account for much of the growth of health care spending" and the effect varies significantly from country to country.[105] Countries have had significant numbers of their citizens in the oldest age groups without bankrupting their public systems. In addition, today's population is much healthier than those of the past, in large measure because of state intervention through social programs, services and regulation. Aaron goes on to argue that the "most important demographic influence behind rising costs is declining birth rates,"[106] because of the impact this has on the ratio of elderly to younger people. The majority of those in the most elderly population, and all of those who bear children, are women, so policy that looks to these demographic factors for explanations of rising costs is necessarily looking to women. Moreover, cutbacks in state support for children and youth limit their chances for a healthy old age, and this increases the likelihood of increasing costs in the future.

Few of these discussions about the unlimited demand for care link this demand to advertisements produced by the for-profit sector promising wonder cures for everything from memory loss to sexual dysfunction, from cancer and infertility to incontinence and hot flashes. More common is a focus on doctors and the claim that they use their power to create demand to enhance their incomes. To once again quote from the Organization for Economic Co-operation and Development document *Health Care Reform*, "government efforts to control costs have been hampered by a reluctance to withdraw the power conferred on doctors to decide what medical care is necessary and appropriate."[107] Various population groups have also been critical of over-treatment, linking this to fee-for-service as well as to the medical model.

Another kind of limit that is increasingly part of health care reform discussions relates to the determinants of health and the impact of health care on health. As Robert Evans, Morris Barer and Theodore Marmor put it in the preface to *Why Are Some People Healthy and Others Not? The Determinants of Health of Populations*, "the effectiveness of traditional medical care as a determinant of health and well-being has been coming under increasing scrutiny."[108] The risk here is that the arguments will be used to reduce investment in health care without either changing the way the remaining care is delivered or addressing the determinants of health inside or outside the health care system.

Technology

Technological change has helped treat more diseases and prolong life. One of the consequences of this could be greater medical costs, because more people survive with significant medical problems that are treated with expensive technologies and care. Women's and other groups have been ambivalent about these technologies, especially in the area of reproduction.[109]

While on one hand these new technologies may create possibilities, on the other, they may limit opportunities for healthy lives, not only for patients but also for care providers. Technologies have an equally contradictory impact on cost. The increased intensity of services is a major factor in rising health costs, and estimates indicate that "one third of the increase in intensity was due to new technology and two thirds was due to small technological improve-ments."[110] At the same time, technologies have helped reduce institutional costs by making more ambulatory care possible. Technologies have also contributed to the shortening of patient stays in hospitals, in that new methods have made possible less-invasive surgery as well as more care in the home.

However, the cost savings could be realized mainly through a shift in care responsibilities from publicly funded institutions to private homes, where it is mainly women who provide the care.[111] In addition, the shifting of care to the home sends the risks of care to the home along with the expenses. Both providers and patients could be at increased risk. Untrained people could inadvertently provide inadequate or inappropriate care. Home conditions could be unsafe, not only in terms of exposure to bacteria and viruses, but also because the environment might be hostile. For providers, lack of training could result in injuries and increased stress. Even those providers who have the skills could find themselves at risk and in isolation, with few technical or social supports.

Moreover, technologies have important implications for how health care is conceptualized, for power and control, and for ethics and access. As Abby Lippman points out in her discussion of geneticization, or the reduction of health issues to genetic make-up,

> While research, services, and policy networks that validate women's experiences as a way to promote their health are set in motion (for example, the five recently funded Centres of Excellence for Women's Health Research in Canada), parallel developments associated with geneticization are likely to present a formidable challenge to maintaining health issues as collective and political rather than individual and medical.

Increasingly, choice in health care is being talked about in terms of consumer preferences and customer satisfaction surveys. The discourse in the new paradigm is that of the market, with talk of one-stop shopping becoming commonplace. In a recent book subtitled *A Blueprint for Canadian Health Care Reform*, for example, the authors recommend that "The Physician should shop on behalf of his [sic] patient to provide the best possible service at the most effective cost."[112]

Health Care as a Business

In *Making a Healthy World*, the authors ask:

> While all history and experience show that public health care must be a public responsibility, and that health systems can only be financed efficiently and equitably by either Bismarckian or Beveridgean principles, we are in the middle of an epidemic of reforms based on various forms of market principles. At the same time, when policymakers rightly question the evidence base of many present-day clinical practices, at a larger system level of policies and practices all over the world we witness sweeping recommendations and reforms of questionable feasibility, effectiveness and equity. Why is that?[113]

Part of the answer can be found in the new paradigm evident in a host of international organizations and agreements. The World Bank, rather than the World Health Organization, has increasingly taken the lead in health-sector development, at least in the Third World.[114] The debts incurred in the wake of the 1973 rise in petroleum prices and changes in lending, borrowing and investment practices left many countries faced with structural adjustment programs established by the World Bank and the International Monetary Fund. The imposed guidelines promote market-oriented, open economies, reduced state support and privatization of services.[115] Even the guidelines for gender-based analysis that are increasingly part of the international package specify privatization as a basic tenet of health care reform.

A paper prepared for the World Bank clearly set out what are described as the "political objectives" of foreign investment in privatization:

- reduce the size and scope of the public sector;
- reorient public administration efforts away from public production towards engaging in enabling and regulatory activities;
- reduce opportunities for corruption and exploitation of public assets by government officials and SOE [state-owned enterprise] managers;
- reduce the influence of particular pressure groups such as parties, the bureaucracy, or labor unions;
- reduce the possibility for a successor government to reverse the privatization process.[116]

The purpose is to transform these enterprises into "efficient and profitable entities."[117]

Another part of the answer, then, can be found in the profits to be made in health care. Searching for new areas for investment and profit growth, corporations have found that health care is in many ways an "unopened oyster."[118] In many countries, most services have been provided by the state or by non-profit organizations, leaving plenty of room for expansion by for-profit firms. Until relatively recently, the United States also had a large proportion of public and non-profit organizations involved in health care. But this has changed rapidly. "By 1994, for-profit health maintenance organizations (HMOs) had more enrollees than their not-for-profit counterparts, which had previously dominated the scene."

Hospitals, too, increasingly became for-profit institutions, often as part of a Managed Care package. Hospitals saw their aggregate profits increase by 25 per cent in 1996, with aggregate profits rising from $5.6 billion in 1988 to $21.3 billion in 1996.[119] This profit growth reflects the movement of large corporations into the health sector and the mergers and consolidations that have taken place as they seek to eliminate competition through both vertical and horizontal integration. In the United States, over half the population enrolled in HMOs are in the four largest firms.[120] Similar patterns are evident in the very profitable drug industries, industries that have been the subject of extensive critiques for their negative impact on women.

This kind of consolidation, especially under a paradigm that favours markets, gives such corporations significant power. In his introduction to a special issue of the *Journal of Health Politics, Policy, and the Law*, editor Mark Peterson points out that,

> At the table of health care decision makers, capitalists–investors, shareholders, and the managers of capital markets–thus demand greater recognition, and by the nature of their activities, wield increased control over both public and private policy agenda.[121]

At the same time, choices are reduced for both providers and patients as firms seek greater control over costs. Their influence is evident not only within the United States but also within international organizations, such as the World Bank, where the US has significant power. It is evident as well in international trade agreements that stress the liberalization of markets, including those covering health care, and that limit state intervention in health services.

Models for Health Care Reform

Efficiency and Choice

All these developments have had an impact on health reform. They have set the stage for a paradigm shift. While reform is not new, what marks the difference between current reforms and those of the past is this paradigm shift: the new paradigm is a business paradigm. It is based on a belief in market strategies and for-profit managerial techniques. It assumes a definition of health as a market good and of patients as consumers. Although it is acknowledged that "the health care sector lacks some of the basic features of a 'free' market," it is assumed that "the introduction of market-like mechanisms creates incentives for improving efficiency, and possibly also effectiveness and quality, depending on the competence and expertise of the purchaser."[122] The imperfections of the health care market can be addressed by "managed competition," defined by the OECD as "government regulation of a health care market which uses competition as the means to achieve efficiency objectives within a framework of government intervention designed to achieve other policy objectives such as equity."[123]

There is, then, an acknowledgment that markets do not lead to equity when left on their own and that not only state intervention but also public financing are required. It is also recognized that "systems based on market principles, notably the United States system, are far from optimal when it comes to allocating resources."[124] At the same time, this recognition is combined with an assumption that competition is necessarily good and results in both greater choice and increased efficiency.

A popular response to these contradictory concepts, at least among those supporting a business approach, is to create an internal market, where funds and some regulation would still come from government, but more would be privatized and allocated by market mechanisms.[125] Within this internal market model, privatization takes various forms.

One form is the separation of purchaser from provider; that is, governments no longer provide services. Instead, they purchase them from competing providers. This is intended to increase efficiency by encouraging providers to compete with each other for the health care market and to provide governments as well as patients with choices. Canada already has such a separation, given that governments do not directly provide most services and doctors are not employees of the state. However, there has not been a tradition of competition among these providers for patients or financing.

There are several problems with this competitive model in addition to the equity concerns acknowledged by its promoters. First, competitive behaviour "may not always make medical or scientific sense, since close co-operation with a broad range of colleagues over a broad range of areas is necessary for good results."[126] Women in particular have stressed the need to develop teams in an effort to address the full range of health issues, and competition could undermine cooperation of this sort. The lack of competition among Canadian health providers has also supported coordination activities across services. Second, competition is more expensive. It increases administrative and other costs, as the American system demonstrates.[127] On the basis of their literature review, Raisa Deber and co-authors conclude that "competition and markets for services perceived as necessary appear to increase costs, rather than constrain them."[128] Third, competition encourages unnecessary duplication. It requires a host of providers who do the same thing and thus means there are extra services that will not get used when one provider wins a contract. Fourth, competition can lead to monopolies, as the winning providers eliminate the competition.[129] In many areas of sparsely populated countries such as Canada, there will not be a range of providers to compete in the first place. Indeed, the problem is not one of selecting among services but one of encouraging services to locate in a particular area. Fifth, competition often means lack of continuity. It can result in fluctuations in the supply of services and in providers. Sixth, the privatization of services often creates the need for greater government regulation, as well as the need for governments to continue to operate in unprofitable areas and provide service for people whom the private sectors avoid. Those most likely to be left out are poor women and people with disabilities. It thus could mean more rather than less government intervention and less choice. Equally important, it could lower quality because "the producer with the lowest price may not necessarily be the one who gives best value for the money."[130]

Another form of privatization–one that could also be classified as a purchaser/provider split–is the contracting out of services. In this approach, hospitals or governments contract out all or part of a service to providers who bid on the job. Contracting out has all the problems of the purchaser/provider competitive model. In addition, there is no reason to believe that contracting will lead to savings in the long run. While competition and the transfer of services to private providers can reduce short-term costs, there is evidence to suggest that this is short-lived. As Starr so succinctly puts it, "the contractors could scarcely be expected to exert less pressure for higher spending than do the much maligned public employees."[131] Instead, contracting may lead primarily to rising demands and increasing influence from for-profit firms. Struthers' research on Ontario long-term care facilities certainly bears this out.[132] Moreover, the contracting out of services can undermine both continuity and institutional memory. Loyalty to the main organization is also made harder to maintain. And while contracting out can increase flexibility, it can also reduce the capacity to monitor performance and reorganize overall service processes.[133]

Partnerships are yet another form of privatization. Instead of, or in addition to, selling state organizations or contracting out services to the lowest bidder, governments promote partnerships between public- and private-sector organizations. These may be voluntary and non-profit or for-profit. The idea is that shared expertise and resources can be brought to bear on service organization and delivery. As Rekart[134] points out, such partnerships can push voluntary or public agencies to conform to for-profit practices. This could have some positive results, but the emphasis may be on cost more than on service, and alternative ways of providing care that have been promoted particularly by women could be eliminated. Partnerships also shift the balance of power. This, too, could be positive and/or negative for providers and patients. The partner with more resources is likely to end up with more power, and this more powerful partner is more likely to be a for-profit organization, especially in the context of a business paradigm.

An additional problem with partnerships is confidentiality. Because they are assumed to operate in a competitive setting, organizations may resist making decisions and information public. Public accountability is more difficult when organizational practices are not readily transparent.

In searching for efficiency under the new reform paradigm, health care organizations are also adopting management techniques developed in the for-profit sector. Indeed, the problems are frequently seen as managerial ones that can be solved through the expertise of managers. Women's groups have been among those concerned about the lack of continuity and integration in health care services; they have also suggested that there was waste and inappropriate hierarchy in the system. Better management could help address these concerns.

However, there is not a great deal of evidence to support the assumption that for-profit techniques are necessarily more efficient or that they are applicable to the health sector.[135] And there is growing scepticism about many of the downsizing, flexible labour practices, just-in-time production and flattened-hierarchy strategies many private firms have adopted. There is, however, evidence to indicate that cost savings are achieved primarily through lower wages, poorer quality care and a shifting of costs, along with responsibility, to patients and members of their households.[136] Private for-profit providers are also less likely to have unionized staff and often hire part-time or casual labour.[137] This should not be surprising, given that most service costs are labour ones, and that for-profit firms need to add profit to their bill. Equally important, their efficiencies are sometimes achieved through a denial of care, or through a careful selection of the least demanding patients. In short, the savings result more from paying the mainly female care providers less, offering them less training, or transferring care to the unpaid, usually female, providers in the home than they do from eliminating waste.

Central to the new paradigm is the notion that governments should not do what the private sector can do. Combined with pressure to cut government expenditures and eliminate unnecessary care, this idea has led to state withdrawal from some areas of care and to the failure of governments to cover some new areas or technologies that have emerged. In the absence of the state, private and often for-profit organizations move in to fill the gap. This form of privatization goes beyond the purchaser/provider split because the cost is borne entirely either by private insurance or by the individual.

Effectiveness and Accountability

Just as governments have increasingly looked to market mechanisms and market management for solutions to perceived problems with efficiency and choice, so too have they looked to market mechanisms and the for-profit sector for methods designed to increase effectiveness and accountability.

One such method is the use of direct payments for services, variously called co-insurance, co-payment, cost-sharing or deductibles. The assumption is that patients will value services more and use them more wisely if they have to pay something for the service. User fees are thus supposed to reduce abuse while bringing more money into the system. In a similar vein, parallel private and public services are promoted as a means of reducing waiting lists, making the rich pay and increasing resources in the public system. Economist Robert Evans refers to such user fees as "zombies," strategies that were destroyed long ago but keep rising again in spite of their inadequacy.[138]

A series of Canadian studies has demonstrated that user fees neither reduce abuse nor lead to more effective use of health services.[139] The main reason is that,

> health care isn't like other products and the "market" for health care cannot be analyzed the same way as the market for shoes and VCRs...people do not often have sufficient notice in advance to make correct judgements about necessity. This is precisely why they consult physicians.[140]

What user fees do is tax the sick, the disabled and the frail elderly, the majority of whom are women and many of whom are poor. They increase administrative costs and bureaucratic processes, and sometimes put more money in doctors' hands, without changing much about the way health care is delivered.

Nor do parallel private and public systems reduce costs, bring more money to the system or even increase access. Research in Manitoba on cataract surgery found that private providers served to increase costs without significantly improving access to the service. Moreover, they tended to decrease efficiency, at least in terms of physicians who worked in both the private and public systems.[141] British research indicates that "far from improving access, privately financed care appears to worsen it."[142]

Another important approach to effectiveness that has emerged in recent years is evidence-based decision-making. Throughout the OECD countries, there is an increasing stress on scientific evidence and on accountability defined in terms of numerical measurement. In the new paradigm, "effectiveness means doing the right thing, at the right time and in the right way," based on the assumption that it is possible to determine scientifically precisely what that is.[143] Managerial practices assume that "if you can't measure it you can't manage it," based on the assumption that everything that is important can be counted and can be counted accurately.[144] What matters in health care is what can be counted, measured or determined through randomized trials. Management science is united with medical science to allow greater control over providers and patients alike.

There is little dispute that such evidence is essential in both clinical and policy decisions. However, what constitutes evidence is much more contentious, as are the problems or areas addressed, the definitions as well as the methods used, and the conclusions drawn. Two kinds of evidence are privileged in health reform. The numerical data measure such things as the numbers of beds and nurses per capita, such processes as length of stay, required nursing time and outcomes, and such attitudes as patient satisfaction. But no number is innocent, as Deborah Stone so succinctly put it.[145] What is counted, how it is counted, how the results are processed and what is done with what is found are value-laden choices, ones that are frequently biased against women or at least fail to take their interests, their locations and their critiques into account. Indeed, the very privileging of quantitative data conflicts with gender-based analysis. w/ qualitative data of OA lived experience / hosp'ts

The second kind of privileged evidence is clinical. Here the gold standard is the randomized clinical trial. But as those who argue for gender-based analysis have demonstrated, too often the standard has been set based on trials conducted with 70-kilogram men.[146] More attention has been paid to this bias than to the bias in the numerical data, perhaps because it is so obvious. However, efforts to address the problem too often have been restricted to including women in trials, and the biases that arise from problems in selection, methodologies and the categories used for analysis have been a much less frequent concern.[147]

Yet both kinds of evidence are assumed to be objective. Central to gender-based analysis is a critique of objectivity, both as an ideal and as a practice. Of course, feminists are not alone or even original in their contention that all evidence is socially constructed by social beings, based on culturally bound notions of value and limited by the particular context in which the evidence is developed. What is much less common is the positive value feminists place on recognizing the locations of the researchers, their personal experiences and the knowledge they have acquired though experience. Nor are feminists original in their suspicion of numbers. Like other critical theorists, feminists have recognized the complexity of social phenomena and have attached particular importance to the context in which data are collected. Feminists move beyond the kind of criticism such theorists make, however, when they stress the gender-specific nature of the scientific gaze and the critical aspects of health and care rendered invisible by the emphasis on quantitative methods.[148]

Critics of current reforms do not reject evidence, nor do they restrict concepts and methods for evidence gathering to those associated with qualitative approaches. Indeed, calls for reform often draw on quantitative sources to demonstrate the need for change. For example, statistics have been used in gender-based analysis to establish the female domination of care work, the connections between reductions in public services and the expansion of women's unpaid care work, the preponderance of women among patients and among those who provide care to family members, and the unequal position of women in the health care field. Statistics have also been used to reveal the systemic discrimination imbedded in the market and to show that women enjoy better access in public health systems. The critics of current reforms see "the pursuit of precision alone, without richness, as a vice," as Julie Nelson nicely put it in another context.[149] From this perspective, there is rarely a single right thing to be done, or a single right way or right time to do it.

The issue in evidence-based decision-making is larger than the problem of limited methods and subjects. It is also the transformation of the evidence available into formulas for care. Such formulas not only undermine the provider's decision-making power—as indeed they are often intended to do—they also increase the likelihood that equity will be defined in terms of sameness, with everyone subjected to uniform care. Feminists in particular have stressed the importance of recognizing context, differences, history and values in making the health care decisions that are as much art as science. Within the context of a business paradigm, evidence may be used more to control and limit than it is to improve the quality of care based on individual locations and choice.

Basing everything on evidence has the additional risk of transforming what are political choices into technological ones to be made by experts; in other words, to revert to the model of which women and other reformers have been so critical in the past. There is, of course, a problem with stressing diversity and individual decision-making to the extent that no generalization is possible. "But we need to ask which women, and which doctors." In gathering evidence, "the issue then is not that all intervention is bad but rather what kind of intervention was involved, when, for what reasons, on what women and performed by whom."[150] Context and differences, as feminists in particular have emphasized, must always matter. The evidence should then be used as the basis for decision-making, not as the decision itself.

Summary

At the international level, the new business approach to health reform has picked up on the critiques of medicine that pointed to ineffective practices and to the limits of health care. The critiques have been used to justify privatization, cutbacks in both public-sector funding and services, and the new emphasis on evidence-based decision-making. Yet at the same time, the evidence on the inadequacies of for-profit care has been largely ignored in the rush to privatization. The consequences could well be bad for our health.

Chapter 2
Canadian Reforms

Canada has been an active participant in these international developments in the way health care is managed, sharing many of the assumptions and values that are central to the new paradigm. Like other nations, Canada has been faced with a large and growing public debt, along with large and growing health care costs. By 1995, the debt load represented 26 per cent of federal spending, while "federal program spending net of transfer payments was only 19 per cent."[151] Provinces and territories, too, had debts and deficits, and a much bigger share of their budgets went to health. Such debts have been an important catalyst in, and justification for, reform.

The solutions in Canada, like those internationally, were sought in market and management mechanisms. As Gene Swimmer put it in *How Ottawa Spends*, the cuts

> have been portrayed as a change in philosophy toward reducing the role of the federal government by devolving responsibilities to other levels of government and to the private and voluntary sectors; reducing transfer payments to provinces, individuals, and businesses; applying

private sector management techniques to those federal government activities that remain.[152]

Like the authors of *Reinventing Government*, the Canadian federal finance minister has made a commitment to "getting government right."[153] The Program Review undertaken by all government departments had a "partnership test" that asked, "What activities or programs should or could be transferred in whole or in part to the private or voluntary sector?"[154] Provinces such as Alberta and Ontario went further than the federal government in stressing that individuals should be responsible for their own welfare.[155] Governments in all jurisdictions in Canada, however, have regularly reaffirmed their commitment to the *Canada Health Act*. Paradoxically, "getting government right" through private-sector managerial strategies and some privatization has frequently been presented as the only way to save the public system in the face of rising costs, rising demands and the limits of care. But in the platforms of political parties there remains a significant remnant of the philosophy that guided the welfare state, and women, especially, continue to show strong support for their public health care system.

International Agreements

State support for trade liberalization and privatization, combined with a continuing commitment to some form of public involvement in health care, is evident in the negotiation of trade agreements.

There is, it should be said, some disagreement about the extent to which health care falls under the trade agreements. According to Judy D'Arcy, who as president of the Canadian Union of Public Employees represents a large number of female health care workers, the Free Trade Agreement (FTA),

> explicitly allows for American private sector management of all hospitals (general, children's, psychiatric, or extended care), ambulance services, various types of clinics, nursing homes, homes for the disabled, single mothers and the emotionally disabled, together with all aspects (i.e., not just the management) of other social services like medical labs…[156]

The FTA permits the management of any public health care service by American-owned profit-making groups, even when most of the money still comes from the Canadian taxpayer.

Monique Bégin, former minister of Health and Welfare Canada, has argued that this part of the FTA means that "any American business could come and buy Canadian hospitals and take over their management. Hospitals are not government services and are not excluded from the free trade agreement."[157] In areas such as nursing homes, rehabilitation services and medical laboratories where for-profit services are already established, the door is wide open to American firms. Indeed, such corporations have moved quickly to expand in all these areas. In an article on the North American Free Trade Agreement (NAFTA) and medicare, Colleen Fuller[158] maintains that private management firms have not yet taken over the hospital sector in the wake of the FTA, primarily because the *Canada Health Act*'s requirement for public administration has provided some protection against such inroads. However, with the federal government reducing funding for health care, and combining it with post-secondary education and social assistance funding through the Canada Health and Social Transfer, the *Canada Health Act* is becoming more and more difficult for the federal government to enforce. Without significant federal funding designated specifically for health care, the *Canada Health Act* could provide less protection against for-profit takeovers in the future.

While the federal government was altering the funding for health care, it negotiated a free trade deal that supersedes the provinces. NAFTA "will eventually bind provincial and municipal levels of government to its rules."[159] The proposed Agreement on Internal Trade was intended to help this process by eliminating trade barriers among provinces. Under such an agreement, opening one province to for-profit American firms could mean that every province was open to such business. British Columbia has been particularly hostile to this development, fearing that a move by one province to welcome for-profit health care or professional groups would mean that no province could resist.[160]

Although NAFTA seemed to protect areas designed for a public purpose, it also set up a process to review excluded services, such as health, "to determine the extent to which they constitute indirect subsidies to Canadian traders."[161] Given that cars cost more to produce in the United States in large measure because of health care benefits for auto workers, it is more than possible that Canadian medicare could be defined as an unfair subsidy. Under NAFTA, governments had until March 31, 1996, to submit a list of programs and services they wanted to shield from NAFTA rules. Fearing that market principles would prevail in the very lucrative health care field, the Canadian Health Coalition launched a campaign to protect medicare. The Coalition was joined by several provincial governments, but perhaps the most effective advocacy came from a legal opinion commissioned by the coalition. Bryan Schwartz, an advocate of free trade, challenged the federal claim that health care would be protected under NAFTA. According to this Winnipeg professor of law,

> To the extent that NAFTA applies to a health sector, it would permit for-profit U.S. enterprises to enter and operate in Canada. Annex II of NAFTA shields health care from the full force of NAFTA, but only to the extent that "it is a social service" that is maintained or provided "for a public purpose."[162]

As long as services are fully funded from the public purse, they might be protected. As soon as services are delisted or even when user charges are allowed, "NAFTA may guarantee the right of U.S. commercial enterprises to enter the market or expand their presence."[163] The grey areas, such as physiotherapy, that involve both public and private money are particularly at risk. This opinion was supported by Barry Appleton, a Toronto-based international trade lawyer, and by a variety of community groups.

The campaign by this Coalition of church groups, seniors' organizations, student federations, anti-poverty organizations, women's organizations and unions was successful in drawing attention to the danger of the reservation clause. In response, the federal government entered negotiations with the NAFTA partners to reach agreement on the general reservation. According to this agreement, all reservable provincial and state laws and regulations, with the exception of financial services, are protected under NAFTA. Existing public health and social services are to be excluded from NAFTA foreign investment rules, so the individual services did not have to be specified before the March 31 date. The letter of agreement demonstrated that the trade deals are not irrevocable, and it demonstrated that politics can make a difference. But it did not provide any protection from privatization within Canada, nor did it protect these privatized services from NAFTA rules. According to former senior Canadian government trade negotiator Mel Clark,

> For practical purposes, NAFTA gives the United States the absolute right to countervail any Canadian export on the grounds that its production was subsidized by medicare, and that this right nullifies the imprecise, conditional limited Canadian rights contained in Annex I and II of NAFTA.[164]

Trade liberalization, as Marjorie Cohen,[165] in particular, has demonstrated, has an impact on whether women have paid work, and what kind of paid work they have. It can also have an impact on whether or not they have access to health care, and on what kind of care they access.

The liberalization push did not end with NAFTA. Canada was also an active participant in the attempt to introduce the Multilateral Agreement on Investment (MAI). The definition of investment included subsidies to health care, education and child and elder care. "By signing the MAI, nation states would cede the right to regulate foreign corporations in all these areas."[166] For now, at least, this agreement is on hold, at least in part as a result of protests from various citizen groups around the world, not least the Council of Canadians headed by Maude Barlow.

Downsizing and Devolution

The federal government has led the way in downsizing. The provinces have followed suit, especially in the wake of the cuts in federal transfer payments to the provinces when support for health, education and social services were rolled together and dramatically reduced in the 1995 Canada Health and Social Transfer.

Government cutbacks on public-sector employment and wage controls have had a profound philosophical impact, and a profound impact on the gender balance of employment.[167] Five major industries (government services, communications and other utilities, education, health, and social services) account for more than 93 per cent of female public-sector employees and over three quarters of all unionized female workers.[168] These industries have provided women with most of their best jobs. Union members are more likely to have full-time permanent employment and, when they do have part-time jobs, to have more hours of work each week.[169] Their wages and benefits are significantly better than those of non-union employees, and those of public sector workers are significantly better than those offered in the private sector.[170]

Although many of these women in the broader public sector are not direct employees of the state, they are often lumped together with government employees. Tax dollars pay most of their wages, even when their employer is a for-profit organization. In making cuts in the public sector, the federal government has established a model for reform that is undermining many of the gains women have made and has reinforced a philosophy that blames public-sector employees. Some of the provinces have gone further, and even taken a lead in undermining labour gains and thus women's advancements through the public sector. And there is evidence already that the result is both job and wage loss as the public sector becomes more like the private one.[171]

Federal cutbacks to health started long before those in the civil service. The federal government began reducing its financial contributions to health care just a decade after public medical insurance was introduced. In 1977, the Liberal government moved away from the commitment to pay half of all provincial costs, introducing instead a formula designed both to make the contribution more predictable and to reduce the federal contribution. The Established Program Financing scheme put a limit on the rate of growth but continued to allow for some increase and to equalize payments among provinces. It also expanded the definition of care to make it possible for provinces to include more than hospital and doctor expenses. In 1986, and again in 1989, the Conservative government further limited transfers. A total freeze was introduced in 1990. An absolute reduction came in 1995, when the Liberal federal government announced the Canada Health and Social Transfer. The introduction of the transfer meant that it was no longer possible to determine how much the federal government contributed to health care, and the provinces received much greater leeway in how they spent the transferred dollars.

In consequence, it became more difficult for the federal government to enforce the principles of the *Canada Health Act.* The new Social Union Agreement among the federal and provincial/territorial governments (except Québec) includes a commitment to the five principles of the *Canada Health Act*, but no enforcement mechanism.[172] The provinces and territories have promised to spend any new money on health, but there is no guarantee that the increased allocations for health included in the 1999 federal budget will be spent in a manner that conforms to those principles.

Provinces and territories have responded to the reduction in federal funding with a variety of strategies. As is the case at the federal level, these strategies do not simply reflect the pressure to cut costs. They also reflect a new philosophy about government responsibility, about the involvement of the for-profit sector and about health care limitations.

In the 1970s, the provinces and territories responded to the new funding formula mainly by introducing global budgets for service organizations. In the 1990s, the strategies were quite different. Reports commissioned in virtually all the provinces stressed the limits of health care and the importance of health promotion. But reform was framed primarily as a managerial issue. Care delivery was to be relocated from hospitals to homes and other institutions, and coordinated, for the most part, through regional bodies and primary care. Both the reorganization of work within institutions and the coordination of services outside them were to be based on private-sector management techniques. The new emphasis would be on what the management literature calls core competencies. In health terms, this meant focusing on "basic insurance services," and leaving the rest to supplemental health insurance, private payment and private delivery.[173]

The strategies could be summarized as "spending smarter and spending less,"[174] with a new emphasis on evidence and outcomes, effectiveness[175] and care "closer to home."[176] In many ways, the various reports picked up on the critiques raised by women. The recommendations for the shift from institution to community, from centre to region and from physician to non-physician seemed to address their concerns, especially when combined with primary care, greater integration, more local control through regionalization and more continuity though integration. Most reports also considered the working conditions and the morale of care providers, although seldom in terms of care in the home.

Not surprisingly, hospitals have been a major target for reform, given their high consumption of tax dollars, the attacks on their practices and their heavy reliance on a unionized, female labour force. A multitude of strategies have been employed, most of which are consistent with the new emphasis on management and on getting government right through privatization. Technologies have helped shorten patient stays and increase ambulatory care and day surgery. They have also been used to reorganize work, monitor providers and transfer labour to workers with less formal training. As is the case in the for-profit sector, hospital services have been vertically and horizontally integrated. Hospitals have also been redefined to focus exclusively on acute care. Acute care has, in turn, been more narrowly defined to include only the most severe diseases or injuries. This redefinition has important implications for patients and providers, not the least of which is a renewed emphasis on the medical model.

All the patients that care providers deal with now are very sick and require intensive care services. As a result, the work is not only harder and more intense, but there is also less time to get to know the patients or feel the satisfaction that comes from helping individuals recover their health.[177] Combined with the managerial stress on measurement and monitoring, the result is often a loss of control for the providers. For the patients, the redefinition means that care under the protection of the *Canada Health Act* is short-lived, given that the *Act* fully covers only hospital and doctor care. Those who remain in hospital for more than a very short period are increasingly described as abusers or bed blockers. Most of these "abusers" are women. As for those who are forced to leave hospital "quicker and sicker," we are only now starting to see the results of research on the impact of this strategy. Given that the extent of public involvement in both the funding and delivery of home care and long-term care varies significantly among the provinces and territories, it is likely to be the case that the impact on women will vary as well. And it will vary from woman to woman, depending on their location, capacities and resources.

Cutbacks in hospitals have significantly reduced employment opportunities for registered nurses. While employment for nurses grew by 36 per cent between 1966 and 1971, the growth declined with budget reductions and came to a halt by 1993. Between 1993 and 1996, nearly 8,000 positions disappeared across the country. And, because these data count nurses rather than jobs, they understate the number of full-time jobs that disappeared. They also understate the extent to which these nurses now work on contract, either as individuals or as employees of nurse registries, and thus with less security and fewer benefits, and perhaps lower pay. During the 1993–94 period, the total number of RNs in Canada remained unchanged, a reflection of both education cutbacks and the poor job prospects for nurses.[178] Meanwhile, more of the work is being done by women with less formal training. Sometimes this is quite appropriate, but the use of what are often called "generic" workers with little or no training could put both providers and patients at risk.[179]

Within hospitals, there is a move to privatize non-nursing jobs. Some of the work of cleaning, food preparation and maintenance has been redefined as "hotel services" and contracted out to the lowest bidder. Such a redefinition flies in the face of a determinants of health approach and the research that demonstrates that good food and a clean environment are critical to health. It is mainly women who do this work. And they have long defined themselves not as hotel workers, but as health care workers, a definition that is more appropriate given the determinants of health concept.[180] Indeed, these determinants are even more important to the very vulnerable patients in hospital care. As is the case with other managerial decisions, this contracting out is only now being examined in terms of its impact on quality and cost. The results available suggest that neither efficiency nor effectiveness improve.[181]

Governments have also entered partnerships with for-profit firms to deliver services previously delivered by the public sector. Laboratories provide one example. The assumptions leading to this strategy are the same as for privatization; namely, that the for-profit sector is more efficient and that nothing that could be done by the private sector should be done by the public sector. The effects are often very similar to those of other forms of privatization: job loss or lower wages for the mainly female workers and very little long-term gain in cost savings.

Regionalization and decentralization have been common themes in health care reform. These strategies have been undertaken in many jurisdictions, on the assumption that decentralized structures will be more responsive to local needs and more effective in care delivery. However, there are important advantages to central planning and coordination, as well as to a collective determination of political principles. "Such decentralization may make the achievement of equity, efficiency, and cost control across the nation less easy"[182] and could serve to undermine the principles of the *Canada Health Act*. It also might make it more difficult for patients and providers to influence decision-making.

The devolution of care to the community has, in some instances, meant more emphasis on clinics providing primary care. Provinces also have moved to provide "one-stop shopping": single entry points for an array of home and long-term care services. Both strategies could be a mixed blessing for women. On the one hand, they could mean more coordinated and continuous care. On the other, they could mean integrated denial. The sole entry point could be used to cut back services as well as to extend them, especially in a context of budget reductions. And formulas for eligibility might apply that serve to exclude many women, especially if these formulas fail to take important differences among women into account. Equally important, local authorities with shrinking budgets might have to sacrifice the traditional public health measures that have been so important to improving health in favour of responding to the immediate demands for home and long-term care. Indeed, there is little evidence of new initiatives in the areas of traditional public health and some talk about privatizing services such as supplying water as a means of bringing more money into local governments.

The last link in the devolution chain is the home, a place where women do most of the labour. Diseases and treatments that were once restricted to institutions on the grounds that they required skilled care in a special environment have been transferred to the home, with mixed results for patients and providers. The transfer of care to the home is often presented not simply as a cost saving measure, but also as a response to people's preferences and as a means of providing more holistic care. But in their study of home-based care, Frederic Lesemann and Daphne Nahmiash conclude that

> these systems are under considerable pressure to resolve the finan-
> cial constraints of large hospital institutions. Such pressure is
> unnatural for services which promote a different rationale for care
> and caregiving. It discourages a family and community dynamic
> which would pursue objectives of health, quality of life and well-being
> rather than respond to pathological problems and services caught
> up in the spiralling costs. If the institutional rationale does not

undergo a major shift, the relief provided by the home care system to this clientele may only be temporary.[183]

Similarly, Sheila Aronson and Jane Neysmith found that "home care workers' ability to deliver high quality, personalized care is compromised by organizational practices that speed up and intensify their work."[184] It is also compromised by the low value placed on the work, a valuation that reflects both the setting of the job and the sex of the workers. In other research, on home care for the elderly, the same authors maintain that

> the historical record suggests that it will be women from low income households who will be hired to provide most home care services. Thus the greatest risks will be carried by frail old persons and low income workers. In other words, it will be marginalized groups of women who both deliver and receive the programs.[185]

Especially in large metropolitan areas, these home care workers are often immigrant women who must deal daily with "racist attitudes and behaviour from clients and their families."[186] And like other home care workers, they deal with the problems of isolation that expose them to the risk of violence and injury.

Many of these home-care workers are employed by for-profit firms. Some forms of for-profit home-care have always existed for private purchase, but provincial governments have been experimenting with funding more for-profit care, even in the face of evidence indicating that such care is significantly more expensive than that provided by government agencies.[187]

Although many patients might well prefer their own homes to the increasingly oppressive hospital environment, we cannot assume this to be the case for everyone. As feminists have long made clear, for a significant number of women homes are not havens in a heartless world.[188] There are far too many women without safe homes to go to once they are discharged from institutions, and a larger number do not want to burden their daughters, mothers or partners even when they have safe homes, and such homes are clean and comfortable. Many men also do not have homes that are safe in terms of what the determinants of health literature tells us are essential ingredients to well-being. Men, too, may resist forcing their children to provide care. A Montréal study concluded that "maintaining the elderly in the community at all costs might in fact be at the expense of their caregivers."[189] The same might be said of all caregiving, most of the providers of which are women. Caring is expensive for women and might be expensive for the system in the long run if the caregivers themselves become ill as a result.

Yet another kind of devolution is evident in the health care provisions for Aboriginal peoples. Here the federal government has been transferring care services to the control of Aboriginal peoples themselves. Provinces too have been transferring control, or at least including Aboriginal peoples in decision-making bodies and developing strategies to make care delivery more culturally sensitive.[190] It remains to be seen whether these services will have sufficient resources, and whether those resources will allow sensitivity to Aboriginal health issues.

Regulation, Liberalization And Partnerships

Consistent with international developments, Canada has combined the removal of regulations in some areas with the creation of more regulation in others. Drug regulation provides a good example.

As a result of trade negotiations, the Conservative government introduced Bill C-91 in 1993. This legislation eliminated compulsory licensing that had allowed any company to manufacture and sell patented drugs once the companies that developed them had enjoyed several years of exclusive sales. Under compulsory licensing, the company with the patent received a royalty to compensate for research, development and lower profits. Compulsory licensing was introduced after research demonstrated what the Québec Royal Commission had termed "the abusive prices of drugs" resulting from both foreign control of the drug industry and "a form of collusion in price setting."[191] Under compulsory licensing profits remained high, but pressure to remove this limit on patents remained strong.[192] First in 1987, and then again in 1993, Canada extended patent protection to brand-name drugs for at least 20 years. Paradoxically, in the wake of free trade, pharmaceutical companies have been granted extensive monopolies through heavy state intervention.

The trade agreements have already had an impact on access to drugs by raising prices.[193] The effect of such patent legislation "is to limit competition and raise prices, and industry profits, thus contributing to the overall escalation of health costs in Canada."[194] Some of these increased prices are paid for with tax dollars, given that the *Canada Health Act* requires that medications necessary during hospital stays must be covered by the public plan. But drugs are one of the factors making shorter hospital stays and more day surgery possible. And dehospitalization means more of the costs of drugs are covered by individuals, either through their insurance companies or out of pocket. As the National Forum on Health, the group appointed by the prime minister in 1994 to look at the future of health care, reports, private drug insurance is correlated with income. Only 7 per cent of those earning less than $20,000 per year have private insurance to cover drug costs.[195] In 1995, 56 per cent of all women with labour-force income earned less than $20,000.[196] It is women, then, who are most likely to have to pay the full cost of these rising prices themselves.

Some provinces have responded to rising drug prices by introducing drug plans that favour both bulk purchasing and the least expensive drugs, with demonstrated usefulness. The "reference-based pricing" system in British Columbia has helped to increase access and reduce costs, especially for the most vulnerable patients.[197] In addition, all provinces have long covered at least part of the costs of drugs for those on welfare and for the elderly, most of whom are women. However, the National Forum on Health concludes that governments are not doing enough to provide access to essential drugs, control drug costs or encourage pharmaceutical research.[198]

The forum also concluded that it is the pharmaceutical firms, rather than the government, that are doing the steering in terms of research. According to the Forum, "'Partnerships' between the industry and particular granting agencies do not help; their research focus is still on drugs. The transfer must be arms length, with no strings."[199]

It could well be the case that strings are attached in many partnerships, partnerships that are increasingly promoted by governments as the way research should or even must be done. Combined with the reductions in allocations for research and for educational institutions, the emphasis on partnerships might encourage researchers to shape their agendas to those of the partners with the money. The new money for health care research announced in the 1999 federal budget might help encourage independent research, but not if the pressure to form partnerships means that patients and health care providers help only to row a boat steered by pharmaceutical and other for-profit firms. Indeed, the single entry point proposed for research funding could mean integrated denial rather than new access for those researching from a critical perspective.

While trade liberalization has meant more regulation of drugs, it has promoted the freer movement of health care professionals across the border between Canada and the United States. NAFTA made "temporary status in the United States much simpler and quicker to obtain."[200] And temporary status "has become a back door to permanent emigration." According to research conducted for the C.D. Howe Institute, the number of nurses who emigrated to the United States in 1993–94 was equal to 40 per cent of the 1991 graduating class.[201] With thousands of nursing jobs disappearing in Canada, many of these nurses had little choice but to leave their country. It should be noted, however, that Canada is more selective, and less liberal, when it comes to admitting nurses from countries other than the United States.[202]

Provinces and territories have also been looking at the regulation of health professions and labour unions. In terms of professions, the tendency seems to be towards deregulation. More public input into the regulation of professions has been a common theme, as has change in the scope of practice legislation to reduce professional monopolies in particular areas. The introduction of midwifery legislation is one example. As is the case in many areas, there are contradictory possibilities in these developments. On one hand, reformers have long argued for greater control over medical practices; registered nurses have long argued that they could do much of what physicians do, and licensed or registered practical nurses have argued that they could do some of the work now done by RNs. On the other hand, the consequence could be that managerial decisions become more important than professional ones and that the lowest-skilled or lowest-paid workers are used to do a job.

In terms of unions, the tendency seems to be towards more regulation, or at least towards limits on union practices and scope. And unions could be further undermined by the contracting out of previously unionized work to the private sector, where regulations and conditions make unionization more difficult. Moreover, some of the legislative protections, such as pay equity, that women have won apply only to the public sector, so privatization could move women out from under the protection of some rights legislation as well.

Like the federal government, other jurisdictions have been extending regulations in some areas and liberalizing them in others. For example, Ontario has introduced compulsory competitive bidding to certain aspects of home care, and this bidding is accompanied by an extensive set of regulations designed to ensure that the for-profit sector has a place in care provision. And, while the Ontario government removed employment equity legislation in the name of reducing state intervention, it also established a commission with the power to close non-government-owned hospitals. Similarly, the expansion of home care also expanded the rights of the state to require information from individual households and to inspect household finances as well as domestic arrangements.

Health protection activities offer another example of deregulation. The federal government has reduced the size and scope of the Health Protection Branch. With fewer researchers employed by the government to assess the safety of food, drugs, air, water and technologies, the government relies more on the organizations producing those products for evidence of their risks and effectiveness, and more on the corporations' financial contributions to fund the investigations. But again, popular pressure from various groups might be forcing the government to reverse field. The 1999 federal budget did contain provision for the restoration of some of the Health Protection Branch cuts, though it remains to be seen how it will spend the funds.

Some of the provinces have taken similar actions in areas under their jurisdictions. Deregulation, cost recovery or the failure to take action in areas such as genetically altered products and new technologies, creates particular risks, ones that have a differential impact. Health Canada, for example, explicitly recognized the gender-specific impact in its consultations on health protection.[203] But it is unclear how gender issues will be taken into account and, in the context of greater reliance on corporations to police themselves, unclear how the effectiveness of gender-based analysis will be assessed.

Accountability, Information And Quality

The 1999 federal budget promised report cards on the health care system, committing $95 million to the project. The term "report cards" is a short form for what is variously described as an "accountability system,"[204] as providing details on "how well the health care system is working,"[205] as responding to a "need to know more about what we're getting for our money"[206] and as a way to assess quality. A wide range of data is to be collected and standardized, with a view to influencing policy development and implementation.

There is little dispute about whether or not such data could be useful for decision-making in health care. Indeed, a variety of groups have called for more transparent decision-making and better research on quality. However, there is no guarantee that the new report cards will address their concerns, or provide them with the kind and quality of data people need to be informed patients and care providers.

The Advisory Council on Health Infostructure recommended to the health minister that the standards for information systems be set by the Canadian Institute for Health Information (CIHI).[207] Bringing together tasks previously carried out by Statistics Canada, Health Canada and various hospital associations, CIHI already exists as an independent agency intended to "define and adopt emerging standards for health care informatics."[208]

On its membership form, CIHI promises members "influence on the direction of national health care standards" and is described as having "substantial representation from the private sector" on its board of directors.[209] It is perhaps not surprising that private-sector firms involved in the health care or the health information business would be interested in membership, given this promise and the potential for profit growth in the information industry. It is more surprising that they are invited to become members, given the potential for conflict of interest. And, representation from popular groups or from the people, mainly women, who provide care in and out of the home might well be limited by the fact that voting membership requires a minimum contribution of $1,000.

But membership in CIHI is important because the decisions made by this agency are not simply technical, although they are often presented as if they were. How categories are created and catalogued, processed and published can have a fundamental impact on care. So if we are to reach the objective of "public accountability and transparency," as *A Framework to Improve the Social Union for Canadians*[210] claims, then membership in, and the transparency of, the organization that sets the standards for that accountability is critical. It is also critical that CIHI take the critiques and concerns of patients and providers into account.

More information is not an end in itself. Its usefulness depends on context as well as on the kind of information and the power relationships involved in all aspects of its development and use. As Susan Sherwin points out, the new emphasis on information for consumers is "built on a model of articulate, intelligent patients accustomed to making decisions about the course of their lives."[211] As she also makes clear, "We need to question how much control individual patients really have over the determination of their treatment within the stressful world of health care services."[212] This is particularly the case in the context of massive changes in the health system, changes over which citizens have had little control and in which they have had little say. The report cards might serve to provide information that does little to address these issues. Equally important, they run the risk of becoming formulas for care, rather than information to be used in providing care, formulas that replace professional judgement and patient choice while enhancing managerial power.

The report cards also have the risk of transforming what are fundamentally value decisions into expert ones. Women and members of other marginalized groups may be invited onto boards and research teams as experts, and they might be able to influence how numbers are developed. This is necessary, but it is insufficient to take their concerns into account. The choices have to remain public ones and be recognized as value-laden ones, with women and those representing various segments of the population playing a major role in decision-making at all levels.

Although the discussions around information technologies are often presented as if they are mainly about clinical choices, patient satisfaction and scientific truth, it is important to recognize that information technologies are central to the new managerial paradigm in terms of controlling work and reorganizing where, when, how and by whom care is delivered. Most of these technologies have been developed by the for-profit sector and they have for-profit managerial techniques built into them. They are based on assumptions similar to those of the medical model, and have all the problems for women that the medical model has. More information can be useful to women, but only if its limits and the value choices imbedded in it are recognized.

Conclusion

Reform is not new in health care. What is new is the context. In the postwar period, the dominant paradigm at the international and national level supported government intervention in the funding and provision of health services, leaving the determination of how, where and when these services were delivered largely to the mainly male doctors who dominated medical care and to the demands of patients. Health care was defined as a public good and a human right, based on a recognition of shared risk and shared responsibility. Undoubtably, this approach improved access to services, especially for women, and allowed for a distribution of care based more on need than on ability to pay. Paid work in the broader public sector expanded, unions flourished there and many women held relatively protected health care jobs.

What was perpetuated and strengthened, however, was a medical model and hospital-based care for most health concerns. The emphasis was on cure rather than prevention, and there were problems with transferring from service to service and with continuity of care. Women's groups and people who did research involving women were among the most vocal critics of health care services, which were not only insensitive to women's varied concerns but also often inappropriate or ineffective. These groups were equally critical of how research was done and used. The research clearly demonstrated that health care is a women's issue, and that all aspects of care had a differential impact on women, which varied depending on a woman's location, broadly defined. Such criticisms have played an important role in the new reforms, as have those raised by others involved in exposing the determinants of health and the weaknesses in the public sector.

The 1970s and 1980s marked the rise to dominance of a new paradigm at the international and national levels. The welfare state, and public-sector workers, came to be defined as part of the problem. Solutions were sought in market mechanisms and for-profit management techniques. Increasingly, health care was defined as a consumer commodity and as a business that can be a source of profit. In the name of cost control, efficiency, effectiveness, accountability, integration, continuity and choice, governments began to intervene more in the organization of health care. Somewhat paradoxically, privatization has often been the strategy or the result.

Privatization has been promoted in spite of a 1985 study by the federal government's Health and Welfare Canada concluding that "the often asserted benefits of privatization were largely absent, or were unknown and possibly suspect."[213] This study focused primarily on privatization in terms of coverage and delivery transferred to mainly for-profit firms. The notion of privatization has been expanded since then–it increasingly involves a reliance within and outside the public sector on market mechanisms. Yet as economist Robert Evans makes clear, "international experience over the last forty years has demonstrated that greater reliance on the market is associated with inferior system performance–inequality, inefficiency, high cost and public dissatisfaction."[214]

Why, given this evidence, are market mechanisms so popular? Evans' answer is that "market mechanisms yield distributional advantages for particular influential groups."[215] These influential groups include the for-profit providers and insurers and the wealthy, who can purchase better access while sharing less of the overall cost. Most of those who benefit are men, albeit a small minority of men; most of those who bear the burden and express dissatisfaction with these market solutions are women. While some of the reforms have improved the way health care is delivered, there is growing evidence that many people have suffered from the reforms and that this is particularly the case for women. In spite of an emphasis on evidence-based decision-making, the context for reform often makes it difficult to deliver care in ways that will take differences into account.

Chapter 3
An "Integrated Continuum of Services"

Introduction

What do these strategies for health care reform mean in practice? How are they experienced by those who provide and receive care? The next three chapters set out to answer these questions in terms of the three major claims of health reform; namely, greater integration and continuity, better accountability and quality and a greater emphasis on health promotion and disease prevention. The answers are provided by registered nurses, the women who provide most of the care; those we interviewed are practising in British Columbia. That province has not embraced the new paradigm as rapidly and extensively as other provinces have. BC has cut care in general, and nursing staff in particular, less than other provinces have. It thus provides a less extreme example of the consequences for care. Yet even in British Columbia providers and patients are suffering from reform. The reports from these nurses provide lessons that extend far beyond their provincial borders.

Integration has become a basic tenet of reform in both public and private health systems throughout the western world. The term refers to a wide variety of approaches but it basically takes two forms. One form involves horizontal integration: the bringing together of institutions or activities that are similar. The most common example of horizontal integration is hospital mergers. The assumption is that bigger is both better and cheaper: better because the focus can be on doing a few things very well and cheaper because duplication will be reduced and work can be done more quickly.

Vertical integration brings together a range of services such as hospitals, long-term care, home care and primary care. The general practitioner acts as "the gatekeeper to the access of medical specialists, hospitals and other elements of secondary and acute care."[216] Here the assumptions are similar to those for horizontal integration, with the addition of the notion that one-stop shopping will allow continuity of care across a variety of services.

The people directing health reform in Canada have accepted both the assumptions and the strategies involved in integration. Canada's National Forum on Health, a group of 24 prominent, and in the main expert, Canadians appointed by the prime minister in 1994 to advise the federal government on ways to improve the health care system and the health of the population, commissioned a paper on integration. The paper assumed that integration could simultaneously reduce costs and promote continuity, although little evidence was offered to support this assumption.[217] It also claimed, but did not demonstrate, that such an integrated system "would be consistent with existing Canadian health goals and principles."[218] The central, and well-known, principles are those of the 1984 *Canada Health Act*: **universality** (coverage for everyone), **accessibility** (the absence of financial or other barriers to service), **comprehensiveness** (the inclusion of all medically necessary services), **portability** (unhindered access to services within and between provinces, and for brief stays outside the country) and **public administration** (operation of each provincial scheme by a non-profit agency accountable to the province).

Similarly, *Closer to Home*, the 1991 report of the British Columbia Royal Commission on Health Care and Costs, established as one of its basic guidelines "the Jericho Process." The term was meant to imply that administrative walls would be "broken down in favour of an integrated system."[219] Two years later, the province's guide to health reform made it clear that an "integrated continuum of services" was "one of the most important objectives of a community-based health system."[220]

Like health care reform, the notion and practice of integration are not new in the Canadian system. For the most part, governments began their involvement in health care delivery by paying for existing services, which tended to be rather disparate and independent. But over the years, governments have used their spending and regulatory powers to coordinate activities and avoid some unnecessary duplication. In addition, they have directly introduced various services that were intended to promote continuity in care.

The idea of making physicians the gatekeepers is not new either, nor is it absent from the current system. Throughout the history of medicare, access to hospitals, public nursing homes and home care has been based on physicians' recommendations. Access to specialists was primarily though referrals from family physicians. There is little evidence to suggest that this is not currently the case. While some people use emergency services for care that might be more appropriately provided by a general practitioner, we could find no systematic research demonstrating that such patients did not have a general practitioner who provided other gatekeeping functions. According to more than one emergency room nurse we interviewed, "actually quite often we'll get patients who'll come in and they'll have used the clinics first. It's not like they've gone directly to the emergency room." Walk-in clinics could also provide a way into the system, but these clinics are serviced by physicians who may have regular patients for whom they perform a gatekeeping role.

Although the idea of integration is not new, the speed and scope of current health reform might well be creating a difference in kind. Certainly this is what the language of reform suggests. British Columbia introduced its reform strategy as *New Directions*, implying that the new managerial approaches would make a significant difference in the delivery of care.

New Directions In British Columbia

Based on the report of the Royal Commission on Health Care and Costs, the Ministry of Health and the Ministry Responsible for Seniors outlined a series of priorities for health care delivery in British Columbia. Five *New Directions* were identified. The first of these was described as a focus on **better health**, which was defined to mean a greater emphasis on the full range of health determinants, on health promotion and disease and injury prevention, and on cultural diversity. The second priority was **greater public participation and responsibility**. This would be achieved mainly by increasing public representation on professional regulatory boards and by providing more information to individuals on self-care. To some extent, this second of the *New Directions* overlapped with the third: **bringing care closer to home**.

Closer to home meant two things under *New Directions*. The first related to increasing public participation at the local level. The health care decision-making structure would be decentralized. Existing community health boards would become community health councils and would include members elected by the public and those appointed by the minister of health. Established at the local level, these councils would assume primary responsibility for "planning and co-ordinating health services, and identifying local health priorities,"[221] in much the same way as the old boards had done. However, the councils would later "assume responsibility for integration and management of services now delivered by the Ministry of Health, hospitals and health provider organizations and resource allocation for the health services in the community."[222]

Regional health boards would replace the old Unions Boards of Health that previously had determined resource allocation within regions and component communities.[223] They would be composed of members from community health councils along with ministry appointees. Initially, these boards would be involved in regional planning and coordination, but eventually would take responsibility for a global regional budget. At the same time, the structure of the Ministry of Health would be adjusted to reflect this regionalization.

The main change with this new structure was the integration of hospitals into the regional and local planning structures. This, in turn, was related to the second part of bringing care closer to home, which was the movement of more care out of hospitals and other institutions and into the home or community. The restructuring of hospitals in particular, along with the transfer of care into homes and communities, led to the fourth of the *New Directions,* **respecting the care provider**. This priority set the stage for a job security agreement between the Government of British Columbia and the health care unions, namely the Hospital Employees' Union, the BC Nurses' Union and the Health Sciences Association. Under the agreement, the work week was reduced and employees could not be laid off during the life of the contract "unless they have been offered a comparable position in a public service, public sector or non-profit community job sector in their region."[224] Pay equity and systems to promote safe environments were also considered important to this priority, as was support for informal care providers.

The fifth and final priority was in fact at the centre of all the *New Directions*: **effective management of the new health system**. Indeed, it could be argued that health reform over the past decade has been primarily about changing how health care is managed. It involves a fundamental shift away from care determined primarily by providers to care determined more by managers, who are often without medical training. In BC, the specific managerial priority makes accountability central. New standards and protocols for the collection of information and for access to the information are to be established; new formulas for funding would be developed along with new means of evaluating outcomes and reporting on health issues. The regulation of professions came under this rubric, as did payment methods for physicians and the coordination of human resources. Perhaps most significantly, the reduction in acute care beds was defined as part of the management priority, with a target set at 2.75 beds per 1,000 population. The creation of "high-quality, effective health services" is also included under this priority, making the focus on management clear.

The commitment to the determinants of health and greater public participation was not very new or very specific, nor was regionalization a new concept. The most fundamental change under *New Directions*, then, was an emphasis on management strategies, especially in relation to hospitals and care providers.

Although *New Directions* shares many goals and strategies with programs in other provinces, the Government of British Columbia has taken a somewhat different approach in terms of funding and human resource allocation. Perhaps most importantly, it has not undertaken significant cuts in health care funding. In 1996, BC ranked first in terms of per capita expenditures on health care. The number of hospital beds relative to the population has declined more slowly than in most other provinces and only one hospital has been ordered closed. The number of registered nurses has actually increased in recent years, while other provinces have been reducing the number employed.[225] This latter trend can be attributed, in part, to the provincial agreement on employment security and in part to the high proportion of RNs employed in long-term care in BC.

Vertical Integration

Community Centres and Community Care

A key element in *New Directions* is vertical integration through community health centres. *Closer to Home* had reported that community health organizations had "little success in establishing themselves in BC," in spite of the "literature supporting their use in particular situations and some evidence that, if they are funded and staffed correctly, they can reduce the number of hospitalizations."[226] The royal commission suggested the active support of such "alternative health service delivery organizations." In 1993, the government announced that new community centres "will establish health teams to provide efficient coordinated one-stop delivery of a wide range of services–from treatment to health promotion and illness prevention."[227]

Like the royal commission, the nurses interviewed for this report recognize the benefits that can come with a clinic organized around teams, and with appropriate staffing and funding. Patients can be treated as whole people with particular medical histories and particular needs. Because patients are known to the staff, providers can respond quickly and appropriately to patient requests for services and information. In the community health centres,

> You walk in and you're triaged at the front. Oh, chest pain–but you're also old and you look pretty lonely. And if you've got a good triage nurse, instead of rushing you off in an ambulance she may say "Well let's do an ECG and let's ask you a few more questions and find out if really you need the social worker because you're terribly lonely." I mean, this happens all the time. I worked in emergency here for six months and it gets pretty hard at 3:00 a.m. to be really sweet to this little old dear who's brought roaring in in the ambulance and you say to her, "how long have you had the cold, dear?" and she says, "Two weeks," and "What made it worse at 3:00 in the morning?" Well, "I was lonely." So if you have these community health centres where they could see a nutritionist, see a social worker, and see the doctor if they really need to and have their lab work done, we see that as in the long run saving some health care dollars.[228]

Staff members with different skills and training can complement and support each other. With multidisciplinary teams, staff members can consult about patients in ways that acknowledge not only that health care is an art as well as a science, but also that caring is as important as curative treatment. And with one main place for care, patients can avoid both telling their stories again and again and repeating tests with each new service. This contrasts sharply with the model of a physician's office, where the only care is doctor directed and decided.

> Right now I go to my GP and he orders X, Y and Z in lab work and then he refers me to the specialist who orders X, Y and Z in lab work and who admits me to the hospital and I again get X, Y and Z in lab work, you know. There's a lot of duplication there but it's all physician run. I don't think that's the way we visualize it, we visualize it as a user-friendly safe place, a comfortable place to go.

The clinic described by the nurses also differs from some of the new clinics being established. "It's still just a fancy doctor's office that's open a little later.

I see a primary health care service that includes a whole spectrum of health professionals. One-stop shopping," offering a full spectrum of services.

To support these views, nurses offered examples from their own experience. Several nurses talked about working in an oncology clinic. The staff, including the doctors, are salaried. The payment system is important because "the profit motive is eliminated. They don't have to worry about meeting their quotas or, you know, seeing as many patients as they can to make the money. So when a person comes to the clinic for an oncology assessment, they get one."

The payment system also encourages the staff to work together collectively, as a team.

> We all back [each other] up, of course...We're all salaried so there's issues about the teamness of it, for sure...When you compare it to what's going on [elsewhere] this is a good model to follow. You know the nurse brings the patient to an examining room and does her assessment. Then the oncologist comes and sometimes the nurse and the oncologist will consult about the findings, and then the physician does his thing or her thing, and then the nurse sees the patient at the end of the visit to sort of...bring it together and see what was said, how it was said. Do we have to pick up a lot of pieces here or...? And then move along and get this patient oriented to our system and what we do and how we do it and stuff like that.

The team involves more than an RN and an oncologist.

> We'll call in a social worker based on our assessment, as needed, and a nutritionist as needed. Some of that is determined by the patient or by the diagnosis. In the follow-up area, that's after the new patient visit, they're scheduled ten-minute slots, anywhere from ten- to fifteen- to twenty-minute slots depending on the needs of the doctor and the size of the clinic. And there again right now nurses bring the patients to the room and in that little amount of time you can get a lot of assessing done. You know, when you have to, you can really tell a lot about a person in a short walk from the waiting room to an examining room. That's all the time you've got. Then you do spend a bit of time figuring out what's going on. The doctor comes in and then the nurse sees the patient at the end of the visit. So there's a lot of contact with the patient.

And the arrangement allows the care providers to adapt to the particular requirements and preferences of the patient. "The length of those meetings with the patient can change depending on...the particular need of the patient...So we've got a new patient visit which [are] scheduled half-hour visits by the nurse, by the physician. They can take longer."

Equally important, the clinic can also undertake preventive work.

And we see women on the breast prevention study, the tomoxifin study. So they don't have cancer but they have a really high familial history of cancer so they come in for regular check-ups and blood work, that sort of thing. And those visits aren't short. Like they're still a twenty-minute visit. There's a conversation that happens in that room, you know, and I believe care happens.

Concerns with Clinic Changes

But the nurses who work in this clinic that now seems like a good model are afraid that the best parts of it could be undermined by *New Directions*. One concern has to do with a different approach to teamwork. Now teams are to be based on a notion of multi-skilling that assumes each kind of worker can substitute for other kinds, rather than complementing them. Instead of having an RN answering the phone, "they'll get a clerk," who will have a new title that will suggest other kinds of training. The nurses worry that clerks will not have the knowledge necessary to adequately assess patient needs. As a result, they could either end up booking costly extra visits or failing to book necessary ones.

Similarly, social workers and nurses might have to share tasks rather than share knowledge based on their own specific skills. But social workers do not have clinical training and nurses lack much of the information necessary to assess social needs. In the nurses' view, this managerial approach fails to recognize the quite different kinds of knowledge required in the job, knowledge that comes with specialized training and experience. In other words, the nurses do not see the clinics being staffed correctly under the new management system, and correct staffing was one factor *Closer to Home* identified as being necessary for efficiency.

A second concern about *New Directions* is related to funding. The payment system promotes teams and care *if* there is enough money to fund the service adequately, just as *Closer to Home* suggested. However, funds are being reduced both because there is less money allocated and because there are more people to serve with this smaller budget. The combination of less money and the substitution of providers means that many of the benefits the nurses saw in the clinic are being undermined.

We're sort of being cut back in money terms as well...So a patient will call in and say, "Well you know I'm throwing up all the time." And so the clerk will just book them the next available appointment. If there aren't any, they'll say, "Come in and we'll fit you in." And we do. And we have treatment rooms for people who are really sick who can't sit up in the waiting room. They're full all the time now.

A third concern involves questions related to access and choice, questions that were also identified as central to the principles of Canadian health care in *Closer to Home*. Under the system that has long been in place, both providers and patients have choices.

You have your own district specified, geographic district, and you run it. It's between you and the patient how frequently you visit, you can keep them on the caseload pretty much as long as you want to, as long as you think care is still needed and that you need to keep an eye on them. Quite often I see people originally when they first get diagnosed and are having chemotherapy and they need maybe some [treatment] to increase their white cell count or something before the next chemotherapy. I mean, you don't discharge them. We keep them on the caseload and maybe just check in with them once a month or something. Or each time they have chemotherapy we go in again for a few days to give more injections, etc....Sometimes I follow people for months and months and months and it's entirely between me and the patient.

This kind of choice for the provider also helps ensure continuity in care.

Those sort of patients I will schedule on the days that I am working. The only time you don't get complete continuity is if it was a daily dressing or someone you have to be seeing daily for whatever reason and on my days off, obviously, other people are going to be in there, but otherwise. And I think that it's one of the very important things.

But these choices are disappearing, or at least becoming more circumscribed, with "constant negotiations and everything." Enormous changes are underway, including proposals to change the hours of work to encourage twelve-hour shifts, with long periods of time off. According to one nurse, such changes would mean "less continuity...because nurses will be less happy." "If you work twelve hours it's very, very hard. And of course you get more days off," leaving patients with long gaps between opportunities to see the same care provider and with fewer possibilities for organizing continuity in care.

As one nurse explained, "We still have choices in our system, in anything, in nursing or physicians." The choices are important not only because Canadians want to decide which providers and which facilities they will use. The choices are also important because skill levels differ and so do facilities and individual needs. As this nurse went on to say, "I don't care what kind of work it is, there's the super-duper ones and then there's the ones that are meeting minimum standards." Or providers could be equally competent but excel in one area while lacking high-level knowledge and skills in another. Or their particular skills might encourage a patient to reveal the symptoms that are critical to diagnosis or allow them to identify particular symptoms not commonly displayed. Choice can allow patients to "doctor-shop" until they find one who can appropriately diagnose or treat their problems. Similarly, facilities might have particular characteristics that serve some individual needs better than others.

A choice of providers and movement among providers and facilities thus could be the most efficient way of ensuring "that people get the right service at the right time, from the most appropriate health care provider," a stated objective of *New Directions*.[229] Yet nurses fear that the one-stop shopping plan that is part of the integration strategy is reducing patient choices with its assumption that one plan fits all and that all providers are interchangeable. If patients have only one entry point and do not meet the one set of criteria for care, then they could be denied access to all care services.

The nurses' concern about restricted choice and access is based on their experiences with the reforms. A nurse involved in continuing care reports that choices have already been reduced, long before the full integration strategy is in place.

> I think in my job our biggest thing is wanting to let people have a choice, you know. We don't want to say, "You have to go to this nursing home." And I think in some cases making a decision, or the outcome of the whole thing, is positive if the person has a choice and can make a decision. You feel that because you wanted that neurosurgeon, you had him, mentally you came through the surgery. That was a helpful thing. Picking a nursing home, if the families can pick, you know, we give them a list and say, "Here's your choices. This is the wait time. This is the time frame. Go and have a look at them. Let us know. You can have only one choice." We used to let them have two…but we did limit it to just one choice in the end, but it is a choice. And I think

it's again that human touch and that feeling that you have some control and you're not just a number going through a slot. I think that really is important.

Another nurse responsible for case-managing care for patients in the community described how choices have been reduced, with formulas developed to limit care regardless of individual need. Cleaning services for patients were an early casualty. Then limits were placed on the services of those who provided other kinds of care.

> We used to put in…a live-in, we'd call a live-in, someone to come to stay with someone for twenty-four hours a day and sometimes we'd have to put in to keep someone at home until a bed became available at a nursing home…And that was again, pretty ongoing; if that was needed that's what was put in. And if it took eight months, well, it took eight months. And you're looking at about $7,000 a month it would cost the system to have a live-in. But there was really no question. And so again that sort of became the norm. And in the community people sort of [said], "Well, my neighbour down the street gets that so I must be entitled to it." So it was pretty well known that that's what was available. Now we're to the point where we have strict [limits]. You're allowed 1,082 hours of what we call "over" hours. So with a live-in you would use that up in about three months. And now we tell the families we can put this in for three months and that's it. So then your options are you pay privately, you pay the difference privately, which would be about $5,000. They're still allowed whatever the maximum is and…depending on the level of care, that's what they're allowed.

But individual differences among patients and unexpected circumstances that are part of every person's life often mean patient needs fall outside the formulas used to determine these limits. The case manager offered a concrete example from her current work.

> I had an elderly lady [for whom] her husband was the caregiver. He went into the hospital unexpectedly so in I came. The family called and said, "Someone has to stay with mother twenty-four hours a day," so we put in a live-in, not knowing what was going to happen with the husband. He died very unexpectedly. Well, now we're into a month of already having a live-in in and the expectation was in two months [the husband would be back home]. This family is grieving…The daughter works. She has her family. The grandchildren are grieving the death of

the grandfather and having a bad time. And I'm coming in and saying, "It's three months now." You know. "These are your options. Make a choice." And we're being told from higher up, like "that's the bottom line."

Choices are also reduced by the combination of more care being provided in the home and less paid care being provided. The community health centres are meant to keep people out of institutions as much as possible, but alternative care in the home seldom provides for all the care needs of many individuals.

What the policy says, like for a live-in or for an extended-care person, they can have 150 hours a month unquestioned. If that's the level they're assessed at, they get 150 hours. But that's only sort of three to four hours a day. If you're looking at somebody that's needing twenty-four-hour care, what happens to the other twenty?

Closer to Home considered the research literature demonstrating that vertical integration could work well in particular situations, with appropriate staffing and funding. Based on their experience, these nurses agree. However, they fear that vertical integration through community health centres will not recognize particular situations sufficiently, but rather will become a single solution that fails to allow necessary choices or adaptation to individual needs. The drive to eliminate duplication and provide a single entry point also might eliminate alternatives and the variety of services needed to provide choices to meet the needs of individuals. They also fear that reduced funding will reduce effectiveness and that new staffing strategies will undermine the advantages that could come with multidisciplinary teams.

Regionalization

Community health centres are only one form of vertical integration, albeit a critical one. Indeed, the changes in home care the nurses describe are related more to vertical integration through regionalization than they are to community health centres. Before the current reforms, British Columbia did have Regional Health Units responsible for the delivery of health services in their areas, although hospitals were divided into Regional Health Districts and remained somewhat autonomous. Many services were coordinated through these public agencies. Under *New Directions*, Regional Health Boards are to be "responsible for regional health planning and service coordination," as was the case in the past, but eventually they will also control the budgets for hospitals, community health centres and other government-funded agencies.

The nurses we interviewed understand the benefits that have, and could, come with greater coordination within regions, but they point out that both

Regional Health Districts and nurses themselves already do a great deal of coordination. A nurse with many years of experience coordinating services among hospitals, other institutions or agencies and homes explained that "It's my job to ensure that the children who require community follow-up, either public health or home care, get it. So I cover the whole hospital and I cover the whole province." Her work is neither new nor unique. "They've had hospital liaisons for probably 30 years, I suppose, of varying sorts and kinds and set-ups. We have liaison nurses assigned to all acute-care hospitals in Vancouver." Working together, the nurses can use their specific knowledge of the patient to ensure continuity for the individual case.

> There's many a time I haven't let somebody go home because they haven't got the patient ready for discharge properly to be handled in the community. And the only one that knows that full well is the home care nurse working in the hospital as a liaison.

A nurse long responsible for discharge planning described her work in the following way:

> It is my position to ensure that everything is put together before you go out the door. And to order things like oxygen to be in the home when the patient arrives or a hospital bed, that's what our liaison does. Or to ask the fifty questions. "Where is this? Have you thought about that?" And not the day they're going home. It's my job to get on to this very early and to be asking, "Have you thought of this? What about this?" And asking the patients the right questions. And setting up homemaking if they need homemaking. There's a thousand things you do. Yes, it's been done at home for a long time.

Under the new managerial strategy, however, some of the liaison nurse positions have been eliminated and the work given to intake nurses. In the process, the complementary knowledge that allowed the old system to accommodate individual needs is lost and the system, as a result, may be less efficient. As one liaison nurse put it,

> I think my questions are very different from the hospital nurses', most of whom have never worked outside of the hospital institution. They have no idea. So almost on a daily basis, for instance, I speak with what they call the intake nurses... In that hospital they took out the liaison nurse, who was a home care nurse, and now they have that same set-up that the city would like to do, plan to do. And those intake nurses tell

me [about] the fall-out from this on a daily basis, and I keep thinking, "Is this cost effective?" This is absurd because the time is escalated for the home care nurses because they don't have proper data. The intake nurses are spending quadruple the time calling back to the hospital to get more information, and even when they think they have it, they don't. Because the home care nurse now has to spend three extra visits trying to put this puzzle together.

This nurse can see how the coordination work could be enhanced by better information systems.

Their idea is that the ward nurse can phone up the unit and tell us what's going on and that she will be one more person doing this. And it'll be on the computer so the ward nurse will access the chart. It'll be on the same computer screen as the health unit and they'll just fill in what they perceive is the correct data and press a button and out it goes to the health unit.

But she is also concerned that the chart will not transmit the kind of information that the liaison nurses used to exchange–knowledge based on the understanding of individual circumstances and community care.

Nurses have not only been involved in liaison for hospitals. They have also coordinated care requests that come from doctors or the community. A nurse involved in case management described how the system has worked to ensure continuity of care.

Our referrals come from the doctor or the hospitals usually, but community people can phone in if they're concerned about a neighbour and we will go out and do the assessment and then determine if they are eligible and if it is sort of a chronic illness, sort of loosely defined, I guess. So the case management part is that we manage that caseload. I'm responsible for ongoing assessments, putting in the home supports. If the home supports aren't working is it time to look at a nursing home or different housing options? So we basically sort of manage their health care needs and, like I say, it's about 250 right now, sort of the average caseload that we have to deal with. And the referrals are ongoing. Like we don't sort of get a maximum and say we can't take any more. I'm in a geographical district and so anybody that calls in, you know, and requests an assessment then we prioritize and see them as we can see them.

The major difference under *New Directions* is that the caseload is increasing rapidly and people are sicker by the time they request long-term care. "They're not going to the hospital. And people are choosing to try to support their family member in the community or at home."

So while the nurses interviewed realize that there is room for improvement, they also want to remind policy makers that nurses have many years' experience providing the kind of continuity seen as central to *New Directions*. They see some aspects of further regionalization as potentially positive, especially if there is genuine collaboration among the various groups involved in care. For example, when a community in northern BC was left with no physicians for three weekends in the summer, the nurses initiated discussions designed to figure out how to fill the gap.

> We sat down with the doctors, the nurses, all the unions, the administrator of the facility, and the Ministry of Health officials and the Regional Health Board. I mean, we sat everybody down in a room and we said, "Fix this problem. And nobody leaves till we fix it." And we came up with a solution that we call "increasing the scope of practice for the nurses," the first call, so that they can handle certain things. The physician will come in for critical emergencies. The nurses get to decide on their own. They get to triage whether it's urgent or not urgent. They get to admit and discharge without changing the legislation. Now this is really, really big news. Because if this is successful, and it's just been given Ministry of Health approval, and this got fast tracked in about eight months in our region. But it was only because we all sat down and worked on it together. The doctors did not feel threatened by this. They want to be able to sleep through a night and not have to come in for Mrs. Jones's asthma, which the nurses know Mrs. Jones really well, or Bobby Jones' fungus foot.

The solution was possible because there was both shared decision-making and a recognition of the particular skills each group brought to the work. While it required collaboration, it did not require any revision of the regulations that govern the various professions. "These are not delegated medical acts. These are nursing acts. They always were. People do not–even registered nurses do not–know what is legally in their scope of practice."

The solution was necessary because the new regionalization has disrupted the way such problems were dealt with in the past.

> And that's the future, because regionalization and restructuring has caused tremendous chaos in health care. And now is not the time to

stand around and be strident and say we're a union, we're a professional association, we're the doctors, we're this. We have to start building bridges. The quality of health care depends on it. So we sat down and we came up with a solution and we bit our nails hoping that the Ministry of Health would go for it, and they did.

Although the union was able to bring its influence to bear in this way on the new regional structure, other nurses saw the new system not only causing chaos but also being much more difficult to influence than the old one. They were simultaneously regulated more and supervised less directly, leaving them feeling somewhat powerless.

We're really affected by regionalization because we were with [another] Regional District and now we're lumped into this whole big thing and we're under massive review. Everything we do [is] being reviewed and we've gone to having…a direct supervisor to having somebody that's way up here. Like we don't really have anybody that we can go to…We're drowning in paper and over-directives from government, and everything's in triplicate and quadruple and you get memo after memo. And we certainly have a lot more forms to fill out.

Contrary to the promises made in *New Directions*, the system seemed more, rather than less, centralized and less "accountable to the member communities" in some ways than in the past.[230] Although the nurses recognized that the new system was only in its initial stages, they were concerned about whether other promises would be fulfilled. Regionalization did not seem to deliver more continuity in services than in the past, even though this was a major objective. As one nurse put it,

I have to admit we're really in early days with our regionalization…that the continuum of care that's supposed to be there just isn't there. And we've got a lot of people repositioned all through the whole system, and for the consumer that's trying to work that system with a demented elderly person at home, it is a really rough journey. Because you keep having to tell your story over and over again. And the hole in our system is our primary health care system. And we've got a division…called primary health care, but it isn't, because the primary health care is the physician's office. And they're not in that system.

She went on to offer an example from her own experience gaining access to the system for her mother.

My mom really decompensated living alone at home, in her own home. She's 86, and we got her referred into the day program…So then we get involved with [this program] and the story had to be told again. She has a gastric problem. We go…to a gastroenterologist and we tell the story again. And each time, instead of her story being passed by her primary care provider, we had to do it. Because the clinical pieces that were necessary and the social pieces just didn't follow her. And mom was too acute at that time to be able to tell her own story. She needed someone with her. Now for an elderly couple in this system trying to get from here to there successfully, and keep intact, it's really tough going. So it's early days, and I hope that some kind of a continuum can occur in all the specialty areas…and the only way it will ever happen is if the primary health care system is folded into the regional system. I mean–and the legislation that's driving this has to change. We've got three different acts that are driving the people that are in the system. And it won't work the way it is.

Although these nurses were still hopeful that many of the promises of regionalization would eventually be fulfilled, they were opposed to the multi-skilling strategy that seemed to be part of regional integration.

And they're telling us that there's a possibility that we will be doing cross jobs. Like right now I'm the one that orders home support. I don't do nursing tasks, but if I'm a nurse why can't I go in and do the dressing and do the meds and set up the home supports, and why can't the home care nurses now that are just doing nursing order the home supports? And we've got physiotherapists ordering home supports, you know. So, certainly in this regionalization they're threatening our jobs. And again they don't want you to be a specialist. They want you to be a generalist.

Some nurses were also concerned that when hospitals are integrated into the regional system the hospitals will dominate in terms of both resources and ideas about care. In the new regional competition for resources, they fear hospitals will win. For home care nurses, the clash in approaches, combined with the massive and rapid changes, is creating a great deal of anxiety. According to one home care nurse,

It's really very stressful right now, the changeover. They don't understand some of the community work. They want us to fit right in to the way the hospital works, and they want us to do all sorts of different ways of doing things. And it's just the inner workings that are different and it's very stressful. The work itself right now is the same. They haven't changed anything about how we operate per se, but how they want us implemented into their systems.

The resources needed for home care seem to have lower priority now. As a result, this home care nurse says, "we're never getting our supplies on time." They tell us, "too bad, so sad. You're in the community. You're last on the daisy chain. The hospital gets theirs and then when they get around to getting ours, we get ours."

Home care not only seems to have a lower priority in terms of expenditures, it also seems to be less valued and less visible work compared to hospital work.

We're kind of finding that, you know, they don't realize, I think they think that we just go and have coffee and smoke with the patients. That's what the hospital attitude is. And it's taken a long time for us to educate them that we really do work just as hard as them and we have to have just as much knowledge, but a broader-based knowledge, than someone that's working on just one floor. And they have a difficult time understanding that.

At the same time, new managerial strategies mean that home care nurses are doing more and more acute-care work. Indeed, "It's almost as acute as a lot of wards in the hospital now. When you consider that they're all getting dumped out early. Those patients that would normally be in the hospital are now at home and we're seeing them." Meanwhile, home care work becomes increasingly difficult for nurses "because they haven't coordinated the cut-backs in the hospital and pushed it into the community. They keep saying they're going to do it but they haven't done it." The nurses now see "really challenging cases" that "take up a lot of our time." So there are both more people needing home care and those receiving care are more needy. "Actually, one of the things that people are saying now is we don't really do case management any more. We do crisis management."

This problem with home care reveals just part of a much larger problem related to the question of continuity and integration across services and regions. According to these nurses, new managerial strategies are creating the need for greater continuity and integration. Hospitals have been redefined to be places where only the most acute conditions are treated, and even these are treated very quickly indeed. In the past, hospitals provided a range of services and varied the length of stay depending on individual need.

I used to work ortho and we'd get old broken hips and through anesthetics or whatever reason, you know, they just didn't come back to where they were. Two months later we were still looking after them. But unfortunately what's happening now is they're sending them out sometimes, regardless. They're just saying, "This person is going home and you're going to look after them in the community." And then we have to battle with trying to find the resources to do that.

Although some people had lengthy hospital stays, most long-term non-acute care was provided in the home. Home care has been part of the health system for a long time, but the transformation in what is defined as necessary hospital care is sending people home quicker and sicker. In the experience of these nurses, this transfer of care can be effective for many patients. However, it can be effective only if nurses have the additional support and training the work requires and if patients have choices about care.

With the increasing use of day surgery made possible by new procedures, new drugs and new managerial philosophies, nursing work in the home is fundamentally altered.

We also see patients coming out of hospital so much faster. The acuity of the patients is remarkable and the biggest thing I can think of is the fact that people come out post mastectomy 24 hours post op. They come out and they've got a row of staples and maybe two drains that they are supposed to be able to manage and of course they can't...Instead of us going in and doing 20 minutes on a dressing, we now spend an hour.

We also have all the counselling...These patients are in shock because maybe they were only diagnosed two and a half weeks ago with a lump and they've gone through all these tests and finally they're out and they're missing a breast. So you spend at least an hour on the first visit because they're usually in the bathroom crying. They're looking at their incision for the first time, etc., etc. And that's the biggest change I see. I think that it's wonderful that patients come out of the hospital sooner. I think community care is great. But I don't think we're preparing them. I think maybe we should have...something that specifies exactly what care they're going to need after, because many people are home alone in this situation. In almost all families nowadays both parents work. Quite often there are no extended family members around and many women are on their own.

They've gone through separation or divorce or whatever so they're coming home and there is no one to look after them. And that's a real tragedy, I find. We spend a huge amount of time, as I say, just counselling them, putting in home support services and whatever.

With hospitals now focused virtually exclusively on curative treatment, more people are being sent home to die. This, too, transforms nursing work in the home and in this case, too, resources have not been transferred to follow the work.

And there's also sicker patients with the palliative 'cause they're encouraging people to be at home. Most palliatives you rarely can get in and out within a half an hour. You're looking at 45 minutes to an hour and sometimes longer, depending on how ill they are and what stage of the dying phase they're in. There's so much more coordinating and you're it. You've got to organize the whole family dynamics and everybody else—all the care. And it takes a lot of emotional strain, and a lot of good judgement in making sure that that patient dies at home with dignity and they're getting their needs met and the family's needs are met. 'Cause you're dealing not only with the patient, but you've got the dog and the cat and the neighbour and everybody else that is part of that dynamic that you have to coordinate.

Along with a redefinition of hospital care has come a redefinition of long-term care. As hospitals reject patients with chronic diseases and provide only the most acute care, long-term care facilities are now doing work once considered acute. At the same time, eligibility for nursing homes has been redefined to cover much of what was once hospital care, as fewer and fewer people are admitted unless they have severe health problems. "The families take care of them until they can't." As a result, a long-term care nurse says, "They're real extended care when you see them." Another summed up the situation succinctly: "Our resident population is increasingly ill when they come to us...We're more like acute...because they [the hospitals] send them back so much earlier. And because they stay in the community so much longer."

Although the workload and the work in these facilities has been transformed, the new planning has not included new resources, new services or new training to help nurses or facilities cope with the new demands.

So we run a lot. It's getting to be more and more acute medicine, is really what it is with palliative care. You talk about palliative care, palliative care is a fairly large element of it as well. It's an interesting combination. But the workload for RNs is getting harder and harder because we don't have, ratio wise, we don't have anywhere near as many registered nurses as in other areas.

Nurses have been running on old experience and old energy, but they feel they have reached the limit on both.

The majority of nurses that work in this setting have got a number of years of experience, clinical and in acute care and/or community and/ or public health. You know, [a] broad base of information and experience. So, many of us have worked there for a long time. So, um, I think that carries us to some extent through what we're doing, what's happening to us now. But we're realizing increasingly that we're just about at the edge of what we can handle. And if we're short-staffed, we are over the edge of what we can handle.

It is not only nursing work that has changed dramatically as a result of these new strategies. The residents in nursing homes now require more physician services, but this does not seem to be part of the new plan. As a long-term care nurse explained,

The other thing that plays into that is that we don't get regular physician visits in long-term care. And you have someone that's turned bad on you, you don't know. You don't have a diagnosis. You don't have any diagnostics, and the only place you can turn is emerg. Because they don't come in. Physicians don't come in. It's not fair to label them all with the same brush, but we need answers so we know what to do next. It's not like when you're in acute care and you can get at least an intern to give you an answer, to write some orders. You're dealing with this acute phase without any proper clinical direction for it. What you end up doing is practising medicine without a licence to do so.

The absence of the physician is partly attributed to the old payment system. Because physicians are "only paid to visit the patient so many times," there is little incentive to accommodate the new demands. "As far as expecting doctors to be there to assist us with the day-to-day stuff, no. We just don't get that kind of support at all. So…when you talk about years of experience it really does count for a lot in extended care."

Horizontal Integration

More dramatic than the changes involved in vertical integration are those related to horizontal integration through the amalgamation of services. This is particularly the case with hospitals. These once relatively autonomous institutions are being placed under the control of the new Regional Health Boards and many of their services are being combined into single centres.

The nurses we interviewed support some aspects of this horizontal integration. They see at least three important advantages that it makes possible. First, costs can be reduced and resources used more efficiently. One hospital nurse spoke for many when she said, "With the shrinking health dollar, budgets and the cost of everything now, it makes sense to me that all the specialists, all the machinery, equipment [are] on one site." Another nurse echoed this view when she explained that "it's utilization of equipment. Like, you don't duplicate." When two hospitals "are both doing cardiovascular, that means you both need set-ups...This way only one group needs it. Only one area needs the neurosurgical equipment, and that kind of thing."

The second benefit these nurses see comes from specialization leading to increased expertise and efficiency. An operating room nurse offered the example of a specific form of eye surgery to support her assessment.

> Well, for instance, we do an eye program for cataracts. We've sped it up so that you do ten surgeries in seven and a half hours. And of course what you do is go to day care, the patient's on an eye stretcher. We bring them in on that and then take them out on that. There's none of this moving from stretcher to table and back again. It's all in one smooth, easy operation.

The third benefit nurses mentioned in relation to horizontal integration has to do with choice. Both patients and providers can have more choice with some forms of amalgamation. As a result of reorganization in one section, for instance, what was once "exclusively the day care recovery setting" has

> now been amalgamated and [the nurses] rotate...And so you admit patients. And discharging patients, [do] the in-between. It does give you a well-rounded perspective of what's happening to everybody—and a degree of fairness too [in terms] of the acuity of the patients, I think...Why should somebody get to work with all the little nose surgery patients and the eye ones and other people have to do all the open heart and the bigger stuff?

Although choices *among* institutional settings are typically reduced by amalgamations, by bringing together a wider range of services at one setting, institutions can offer patients more choice *within* that setting to meet their specific needs and preferences. Because many of these needs arise during the course of treatment, rather than before patients enter the institution, there are clear advantages to consolidating some services. Maternity care provides one example. In a new maternity centre,

> you could have natural birth, Caesarean, whatever you want in that one centre. I really like the idea that this is where you go because this is where the special things are...All the pediatricians are there. The surgeons are there. There's birthing rooms but there's also the Caesarean table...If you want to use the tank, there's also the tank room. Whatever.

Another example of amalgamation that works in terms of offering more choice can be found in long-term care. One institution provides a three-level program. At the first level, residents who can manage most things on their own live quite independently with the help of some support services. If the condition of the residents deteriorates, they can move within the same institution to settings providing higher levels of care. Continuity is maintained and the residents remain in familiar surroundings.

A hospital has also developed a geriatric program that takes advantage of specialization to provide a range of choices designed to build in continuity for its patients. This program was developed before the *New Directions* policy initiative was introduced. According to the nurses who described this example, salaried doctors run the unit with "no interference from the administration." One doctor is in charge of the entire geriatric program in the region, although geriatric services are located at several sites. The hospital offers special rehabilitation services designed to make patients well enough to go home rather than to long-term-care facilities. Out-patient services at different locations have on-site geriatricians "so that if a person is in trouble at home and they aren't managing, they may be admitted there for diagnostics and work-up to see if they can figure out what they can do to improve their level of care for their husband or their wife."

Along with the salaried geriatricians, there was usually a doctor close by. "It was beautiful. I've never worked in acute care like this, because they were on site. You could get your stuff done." The availability of the doctor meant that "there was no waiting." This amalgamated program has been in place for long enough to demonstrate that "We actually did keep people...out of nursing homes for quite a long time." Unfortunately, this example of success-ful coordination might now be under threat because of a focus under the new management structure on short-term costs. "[They] say it was an expensive program, but…it was cost-effective" in the longer term. Indeed, one nurse maintained that the comprehensiveness of one such program disappeared with amalgamation, as an emphasis on finances in the short term replaced an emphasis on the coordination of patient care.

Concerns with Horizontal Integration

As this last example suggests, in addition to these benefits, nurses see some significant problems with the amalgamation strategy. Perhaps most impor-tantly, they fear that specialization and amalgamation will become the only strategies to be implemented. In their experience, these strategies work well for particular cases and particular places, but have serious disadvantages if applied more universally. For example, the previously described maternity centre works well because it serves a small region where "the hospitals are close together." Similarly, cataract surgery services may be appropriately amalgamated because this kind of surgery can be planned in advance and the location selected in response to patient needs. However, much surgery is not elective. When time is of the essence, it might be more appropriate to provide the surgery closer to home. One nurse put the case succinctly:

> I think that in a very technical area, for instance eyes, very expensive equipment is required to do a lot of these procedures. I don't think we can afford to have all that equipment at [both hospitals]. But [that's] because that's a very specific thing. It's an elective surgery…You decide to have your cataract done. It's very controlled. But you do not choose when you have your myocardial infarction, and most people would think if they're having chest pain they'll go to the closest facility.

As another nurse pointed out in this discussion, it is also quite possible that "You could be in the hospital having your hip done and you might end up having a heart attack." Too much specialization that treats patients merely as collections of body parts can make it very difficult to provide care for whole people with complex problems. Nurses offered several examples from their own experiences of multiple problems occurring in specialized centres. The problems could not be treated at these centres because the needed equipment and health professionals were no longer available there. As a result, patients had to be moved to another facility, at great risk to their health. Such moves can mean at least "45 minutes to transport, plus when are the ambulances going to get there to take them? Where are we going to put them when it happens" if the next elective surgery patient has already arrived?

Based on their experience, the nurses recommend that specialized centres be limited to locations close to facilities offering a wide range of services. In their view, integration strategies should take into account the reality that many health problems are not amenable to preplanned interventions, that individuals often have complex and unpredictable health needs, and that many problems can be handled quite appropriately in institutions of varying sizes.

A second problem the nurses see has to do with choice. Although bringing together services in a single centre can mean both more continuity and more alternatives, too much amalgamation can also limit choice. Patients do not want to be limited to one distant centre for the treatment of heart attacks. Many want to be treated closer to home, and thus closer to their relatives and friends.

> The other thing we're forgetting, too, [is that] for you or me to get to [these specialized hospitals] means nothing. I have lots of clients who say, "My husband is in a rehab unit out in the [specialized hospital]. I can't get out there to see him." "The bus doesn't go" or "I can't afford a taxi. If he could only be at [another hospital], I could go up and see him."...The family can't get to see them. I mean, that's a big issue.

Patients may also have less choice in amalgamated systems about how long they can stay in the hospital and about when they can enter nursing homes.

> There's a shortage of nursing home beds...The wait list for [one institution], which is one of our newest ones...it's a four-year waiting list to go there. I'd say the average wait is probably a year to a year and a half to get into a nursing home.

> We have tightened up who qualifies. You have to be on Intermediate Care Level 2 before you can be eligible to be even wait-listed. They used to take personal care at one time. And they don't do that any more. And then, the ones in the hospital... people will come home to wait for placement 'cause they don't want to keep them in acute care.

Equally important, a transfer to a nursing home could limit not only choice but also access (access is one of the five principles of the *Canada Health Act* that *New Directions* promises to uphold). Access is reduced because, unlike in hospitals, fees can be charged in nursing homes. A nurse we interviewed had personal experience with the shock people feel when they understand the conditions attached to what they thought was guaranteed access.

In our job, we're the only ones that talk money. That's the other thing. We do a financial assessment. We look at their income tax and we have a form that we fill out and at the bottom it comes out whether you pay some of it, like it's a client portion. For some people it's zero. For some people it's $2.50. Some people it might be $40.00 a day. It's a daily rate. So, it's subsidized to a point, depending on your income. But we're the only health care people, like I'm the only nurse that ever seems to have to come out and say, "I need your income tax forms. I need your social insurance number. I've got my calculator. And then we've got to talk about finances. The thing is, going into a nursing home it's going to cost you X amount of dollars." And so people are shocked. They'll say, "I'm a taxpayer. I've been paying taxes all my life," and "Health care is supposed to be free and now you're telling me it's going to cost me so many dollars a month to have this help." So we're constantly–that's a big battle in our job.

Instead of the new managerial system saving costs, nurses see the system reducing costs by shifting them to the individuals who need care.

Early discharge and day surgery can also limit patients' choices. An operating room nurse in a new day surgery program recognizes the benefits, but at the same time she worries about reforms that do not allow for variations among patients.

The equipment is phenomenally better. These patients don't bleed. They do so much better. And I think there are areas where it's appropriate. We have anesthetics that are so much better. And we do day care so that patients can go home. But I think that sometimes we push patients out [before they are physically well enough to leave].

A third problem with horizontal integration, related to the first two, is the extent and speed of the changes. A key objective of managerial strategies is to eliminate waste, and any empty bed is considered to be wasteful. Yet the system needs some extra space, some slack, to allow for the unexpected, which is a constant in health care, and to meet individual needs in ways that are integral to effective health care.

Well they think, well, the way it's explained to us is that the reason they're closing the CCU [coronary care unit] at the [one hospital] is because between [a second hospital] and the [first hospital] there's always one or two empty beds. So now they're going to close CCU and amalgamate it with ICU [intensive-care unit], which to me is terrible and I would hate to have a heart attack and then be beside some neuro patient on a ventilator. I don't think that would be too restful for my poor ticker.

According to many nurses, the primary motivation for these closures is financial, not the needs of the patient. But the nurses are convinced that the need is there, and the old service will eventually have to be replaced at greater cost.

They're saying that will get rid of the staff in this CCU so it's going to save money that way. But we don't have enough critical-care beds in the system now most of the time so I really don't see how it saves money in the long run. And besides, what does it matter, you know.

The problem involves much more than uncomfortable care. It can also involve more direct and obvious risk to the patient.

They closed the neuro at the [second hospital] and put it over at the [first hospital] and they kept no neuro instruments at the [second hospital]. So, an ambulance who's told "If you've got a patient you go to the closest hospital" so they wheel into the [second hospital] with some poor head injury. And it did happen. Some person got knocked down at an intersection and was brought to the [second hospital] with a head injury. Well, we couldn't do anything with her, we didn't have any neuro instruments. And they had to put her back in the ambulance and drive her all the way across town. She died. Same thing happened with a baby that was brought in to us. Abused baby. Very badly beaten up. Went up to the OR and they had no pediatric instruments to open the baby up. They did it anyway, but...

There are fewer beds in the new system, but there are not fewer patients. People are moved in and out of the system very quickly, so that no beds and no time are wasted. As a result, each patient requires considerably more care. Management has not planned for this increase in the acuity of patients, and thus in the intensity of caring work, by increasing the number of nurses available to do the work. A nurse who works in an intensive-care unit offered the following response to a manager who had argued that there was no reduction in nursing staff.

I said, "No, you haven't cut but you need one hell of a lot more because, for instance, where I work–in the open-heart area–we kept them for two days in ICU before they even came over to the ward. But now they're sending them out to the ward in less than 24 hours. But you're not increasing the nursing staff as the acuity has gone up." What they want us to do I have no idea. Stand there and say, "Heal thyself"? But I'll be standing there watching you and eight other people to make sure you don't bleed to death...You hardly speak to each other on the shift any more.

I was down in emerg the other day, and the girl was saying they couldn't believe it last night. At one point they only had four patients in there. It was so wonderful. We could actually sit back. And ten years ago that would have been once or twice a week...But now it's just no more like that. And certainly the wards are never like that. You feel good. You feel like you're getting a break if you're fully staffed, and if you have time to sit down and do your charts.

In the rush towards integration, changes often occur without consultation and without warning. The rapidity, combined with the lack of information, creates anxiety among nurses and makes it more difficult for them to provide supportive care.

It's not been a happy thing altogether. In the last three and a half years, we had two reorganizations. The first one essentially resulted in displacing 80-odd nurses and, you know, everybody twirling around and then settling down to a different place. And three and a half years later it has affected 40 of us [in] publicly funded extended care.

A fourth problem with horizontal integration, according to these nurses, concerns the information links among various parts of the system. With patients moved from facility to facility, or in and out of facilities, so much more quickly, the transfer of information about them becomes even more critical if continuity of care is to be maintained. Focus groups including members of the public reveal that this transfer of information should be a top priority.

The biggest thing that's coming back is that there isn't any continuity, and I've got ten people coming in and asking me the same questions. So you know that's true and we have to look at that...Certainly the biggest complaint is that there's no continuity, with nurses, with physio, with home support.

Several nurses hastened to point out that some systems have been working well in terms of integrating the information for patients undergoing major surgery. Nurses who have the appropriate knowledge and who can respond to complex questions from patients about the surgery are designated to initiate phone calls to them.

> We just started earlier this year. It's been going for about six months. Four months? [It's a] same-day surgical admit program for open hearts and some vasculars, and [the hospital] designated a couple of nurses and they phone the patients ahead of time, ask them about their fears, basically tell them what to expect post op. And then the patients come in to them and get shaved and get sent home to save a bed for the night. And then they come back at 6:00 a.m. and they go off to the surgery. And this same program, after, they mark down when they're discharged and those nurses phone them two days to four days post op and just see if they have concerns, ask them a bunch of questions, and I gather the patients are really liking this. And I know it's really helped us on the ward that we don't have so many shaves, shave preps and stuff to do. Those nurses take care of them...And that's great for the families, but when you're down the hall and you've got families calling all the time, it's a real time factor too...We try to have the families there. I'm just talking about my program 'cause that's basically all I know. But I won't show a post-op video, for instance, until the wife or the spouse or the significant other is there because people don't retain an awful lot after being on by-pass.

But these same nurses also worry that new management strategies could mean either that these calls are made by people without the knowledge RNs have or that the calls will no longer be made at all.

More frequent were accounts of the failure to transfer information in a way that provides continuity and avoids unnecessary duplication. Nurses in hospital settings complained about patients arriving with little warning and little information. Take the case of cancer patients:

> But the fact [is] that you do not see the patient's chart until the minute he arrives, the minute they arrive from recovery. And you're just looking to see what kind of drains they've got in and what kind of tubes they've got. Also, we have talked about this many times before and it's never happened. If the patients go to the cancer clinic there is no documentation, if they end up coming to acute care, that comes from the cancer clinic quite often with the patient. If a patient's been kept care of by the home care nurse and been failing at home and they've decided to send them into the emergency because this abscess has got

worse or whatever, there's no papers that come from the home nursing care to say, "Now, this is what happened yesterday, and now this is way worse today." It's only if the home care nurse or the person at the cancer clinic has time to give you a phone call to tell you about this. And then that's in the person's head who took it. It's not written down or anything.

We fax forms to the cancer clinic from the acute care. We fax forms to the home care. We've sent transfer forms with patients to facilities in long-term care. We talk to them on the phone. Really, sometimes acute care is the last place to get information back when the patient comes in.

There were always the progress notes that are typewritten as well as the orders and the allergy record and the [hospital] stuff, and we also send the same documents to home care. What we don't do–and those are all physician-related documents–what we don't do is what we used to call the nursing transfer form. That seems to have gone by the wayside.

Now the transfer of information depends on a nurse finding the time and energy to call. Yet those we interviewed fear that fewer and fewer will have either the time or the energy, and consequently the continuity now provided on an ad hoc basis will disappear.

Information disruption also occurs when patients leave the hospital. Some nurses engaged in community support work report that they

might deal with four or five responsible nurses in the course of that hospitalization. And you start at square one every time. There's no paper trail…to know what happened yesterday or the day before. So [the patients] go through the discharge planning process with you from square one. And for us it's very repetitive because we have to do it so many times.

It is not only the rapid movement of patients from service to service and from facility to facility that makes continuity difficult to maintain, it is also the movement of patients among areas within the hospitals. This movement results from bed shortages in some areas and from nursing shortages in others. For example,

They might be cystics. They have a lot of cystics there. Cystic fibrosis and stuff like that. So for a whole night shift if they only have one nurse who can do the respirators, they will move the patients. They will phone all over trying to get a critical-care nurse, but if they can't find one they will move the patient to a PAR [postanesthetic recovery] setting or somewhere where they can keep care of them.

A fifth problem with amalgamation results from management practices with regard to the allocation of nurses, which can further undermine continuity in care. A number of these practices get in the way of the efforts by nurses to provide continuity by becoming familiar with their patients.

Casualization of the nursing workforce is one of the management practices that makes continuity of care difficult to maintain. These days, very few nurses are being hired as full-time, permanent employees. Instead, they are being hired on a casual basis to fill the minimum requirements in particular areas. Casualization

> means that one day you're working in [one area]. The next day you're working somewhere else. It doesn't mean that at any point in time you're not doing the best you can where you are. I'm talking about continuity in the big picture.

> Employers are not employing people on a regular basis. Because they don't have to pay benefits, they can pay less for holidays...They don't have to pay sick time, they don't have to pay LTD [long-term disability insurance] and all those other kinds of benefits that regular-status employees get.

Although nurses who are employed casually still try to do their best, it is difficult to remain loyal to patients or to institutions under these conditions. As a result, "You lose commitment." And it is not clear that the savings that come from not providing benefits or overtime pay make up for this loss of commitment or for other costs.

The nurses may not only lose their commitment, their health can suffer as well. "The casual nurses I work with right now are burned out. They are exhausted from trying to do this. And they're working at two sites, too...One day you work at [one hospital], the next day you work at [another hospital]." Working at two hospitals can mean both that the casual nurses are exhausted and that they lack the opportunity to know their patients. The quite different conditions and practices at each site can mean that they are not as familiar as they could be with the equipment they must use or with the other nurses and allied health professionals with whom they must work.

From the perspective of a nurse who has to organize casual work, the practice of casualization can be quite inefficient. "Because they are casual, they're not home all the time. They could be at another job. So you start phoning around. They're not all home waiting for a call." When a casual nurse is located, she is booked for an eight-hour shift, and another nurse might be required to work the next shift. Twelve hours must elapse before the next casual employee can work in this particular institution again, or overtime pay is required. This is seldom an option. "I get jumped on from great heights if I bring in somebody and it costs extra." The additional work involved in filling the gaps is not included in the calculation of costs. Nor is the lost care time for patients when casuals cannot be found in time.

Meanwhile, the regulations concerning consecutive shifts do not necessarily mean that nurses do not work consecutive shifts. Moving among institutions, casual nurses can work "more hours than full-time...If you're available, there's work there. If you're willing to do 12-hour nights or whatever." In spite of their exhaustion, the casual nurses take the work when it is available because they cannot count on having enough work in the week, the month or the year to meet their income requirements. Some "work in three places. And no agency gives them enough work that they can say, 'Yes, I will commit to this organization'."

Casualization can also mean that patients see many different nurses, even on a single shift. This was certainly the case for one nurse who herself had major surgery and spent time in an intensive-care unit.

> The first night I was there, they were very busy and short-staffed. It was supposed to be one-on-one. They chose two of us who were the most healthy and we shared a nurse. And on the shift when I got back there at three, until seven the next morning, I had three different nurses because they couldn't get someone to take the whole shift. And so there was no continuity.

There is little continuity, or security, for the care providers, either. Casual employees can be called in for a shift and sent home immediately if the demand has decreased in the interim and she doesn't actually start to work. If she arrives,

> and they decide they don't need me, then they pay me for a minimum of two [hours]. If I pick up my stethoscope and my pen and start to work, they have to pay you for a minimum of four. So they keep you. And if it's not busy there they could float you anywhere...and they've given us more to do.

"That's their right to do that with casuals." The same thing can happen to a regular employee called in to work extra shifts. As a full-time nurse explained, "If I was on a day off and called to work then they could send me home because it's like a casual shift. But they can't do it if you're regular." However, if she went in "to help them out, and at 8:00 in the morning they cleared out emergency and it was all quiet, they could then send me home."

Another management practice, and one that is similar to casualization, is the increased use of part-time staff. Some nurses prefer part-time or casual employment, both because it allows them more choices about hours of work and because it allows them to better avoid exhaustion and poor working conditions. Under the right conditions, such employment can also mean stimulating variety in the work. One nurse explains that she worked this way for many years:

> And I enjoyed it. I really enjoyed it. And I worked when I wanted to. And I worked more as a casual nurse in a sort of a part-time capacity than I do in my part-time capacity. And I had more variety. We're a small facility. We don't have to go off site and stuff like that. But I had the opportunity to go everywhere and not get caught up in the political bull that happens.

But more and more nurses have little choice about taking on part-time or casual employment because, formally at least, work is available only on a part-time basis. "And they can't turn down a shift for fear they won't get one in three days. And I fear the patient suffers, too. I really do." Like casual nurses, part-time nurses may be moved around the hospital or among hospitals in ways that make continuous care difficult to deliver. And like the casuals, the part-timers are often unfamiliar with the workplace and with the other workers. Valuable care time can be lost just finding out where the supplies are kept or learning how the equipment works and who has what responsibilities for which patients.

While continuity is more likely when nurses are on regular, full-time staff, this is not guaranteed. Increasingly, more full-time nurses are "floated" around the hospital to fill gaps, ensuring in the process that there is no time defined as wasted. This floating can mean that nurses work in completely unfamiliar areas.

> They can float you to somewhere else. I got a call last night at 10:30 from the patient-care coordinator. "Can you come to work tomorrow morning in emergency?" I haven't worked in emergency since '89. And I said, "Well, actually, no I can't. I've got to go to a meeting." And she said, "Well, I'm absolutely desperate. Do you know of anyone who works emergency, who's ever worked emergency?"

This effort to reduce care to the lowest possible number of nurses, with gaps filled at the last minute, means, at best, some discontinuity in terms of the people providing the care. At worst, it means gaps are left unfilled, and whole areas of the hospital "are still short-staffed."

Assessing the Goals of Integration and Continuity

Health care reform in British Columbia promises to integrate services in a manner that will provide continuous care while reducing costs and maintaining the principles of the public health system. The key to this reform is a set of new management strategies, implemented at the provincial, regional and facility levels.

The nurses interviewed for this study had a great deal of experience with the old system, and at least as much direct experience as any other group with the new reforms. They were quick to point out that integration is not new. Regional health units and hospitals, along with other facilities, have a history of coordinating care. Much of this coordination has been delivered by nurses working in admission and discharge planning, in home care and in community clinics.

These nurses nonetheless recognize that there is room for improvement; there always is. The nurses are particularly enthusiastic about the further development of community health clinics or centres based on interdisciplinary teams. And they support the amalgamation of some services, especially when services concentrated in one location offer a range of treatments and remain socially as well as physically accessible.

Their experiences with the new reforms, however, raise many concerns for these nurses about continuity, cost savings and the principles of medicare. In their view, the interdisciplinary teams in community health centres risk being transformed into groupings of multi-tasking employees, with the employees being forced to substitute for each other regardless of the specific skills each of them has. With funding cutbacks and new funding criteria, these centres could become involved more in placing limits on care and on choices than in ensuring continuous care. As a result, there is a risk that care will become less comprehensive, in violation of one of the five principles of medicare.

These limits are particularly problematic when combined with the wholesale shift in hospitals towards day surgery and out-patient services. The further patient care moves from the hospital, the more costs are transferred to the individual. The consequence is less accessible care, threatening another medicare principle.

The rapid transfer of patients from facility to facility that accompanies these service shifts also means less continuous care. So too does the concentration of specialized services in large hospitals, as amalgamations increase the distances patients and their relatives must travel. Continuity of care is further disrupted by management practices that move nurses around frequently and that increasingly employ them on a casual or part-time basis.

Nurses are sceptical about the long-term cost savings that these strategies promise. Money seems to be saved primarily by employing fewer nurses and on a less regular basis, by shifting costs to individuals, and by denying them care altogether. In the long term, the result will be more exhausted nurses and a nursing shortage. The costs of this shortage, and of the disruptions in service caused by the new reforms, could turn out to be greater than the immediate savings, especially if the health of nurses and their patients is taken into account.

Chapter 4
Accountable, Appropriate, Quality Care

"Providing the best possible care" has become a central issue in the new health care reforms, and "best" is defined primarily as accountable, appropriate, quality care.[231] Throughout this century, the determination of the appropriateness and quality of health care was left mainly to patients and those who directly provided their care. The health care provider's judgement was the essential basis for appropriate, quality care. Such judgement, in turn, was assumed to be based on specialized knowledge both of health care theory, evidence and practice, and of individual circumstances. Providers were held accountable for their judgements and actions through the use of professional ethics procedures, which were enforced by professional associations or other regulatory bodies to which patients could appeal. Care providers were expected to be able to explain the reasons for their actions to the satisfaction of their peers or lose their right to provide care. For nurses, there was the added constraint of doctors' orders and of direct supervision through a nursing hierarchy. Defining themselves as "patient advocates," nurses were also assumed to be accountable to their patients, as well as to managers.

It is these methods for assuring quality, appropriateness and accountability that reform strategies seek to alter. People "recruited for managerial skill and experience,"[232] along with additional means of ensuring accountability through measurement, are now deemed essential "not only to hold down costs, but also to decide what constituted appropriate care." Managerial science is to guide medical science towards cost-effective care. In this new regime, "*effectiveness* means doing the right thing, at the right time, in the right way."[233]

Increasingly, evidence-based decision-making is used as an umbrella term to encompass this new emphasis. The evidence referred to covers an enormous range. It includes the randomized clinical trials often called the "gold standard" in health care.[234] It also includes "best practices," which themselves may be based on clinical trials or may simply reflect what the average or most common or least costly practice is at the time. Here data on such diverse matters as length of hospital stay, readmission rates and number of Caesarean sections performed can constitute "evidence." Included as well are data on population health that document trends in the incidence of diseases and injuries among specific groups of people. There is, in addition, evidence that is more clearly managerial in its purposes, such as patient classification systems and work-sampling systems. Examples range from diagnostic-related groups (the more widely used term) to Total Quality Management techniques for measuring the time and tasks involved in bathing a patient.

In theory, the evidence is intended to supplement, rather than to be a substitute for, the judgements of providers, patients and managers, allowing them to make informed choices among options based on their knowledge of the specific context and individual. There are several reasons why such evidence cannot easily be substituted for judgement.[235] First, the evidence itself is based on judgements—on decisions about what counts, and about how it is counted, categorized and evaluated. Second, much of the evidence that does exist is inconclusive, contradictory or based on quite limited studies. This kind of evidence is assembled using studies in which most variables are controlled or held constant, while one or two variables are considered, yet the judgements made by care providers often must be based on the consideration of a wide range of variables. Third, evidence about what works in terms of health care is always about patterns, trends and best guesses. It can never reach the kind of precision and confidence levels that can be found in non-human sciences, even when the research focuses on one drug or one procedure and meets the requirements of the gold standard. This is, in large measure, because patients, providers and managers are all thinking, unique individuals, not a collection of standard parts to be fixed or managed in fragments. What works in general might not work in specific cases.

Health care is necessarily an art as well as a science, and neither the evidence nor its applications are free of value judgements. As a result, best practice comes mainly from the use of as much different evidence as possible to inform choices, including the knowledge gained from individual experience and about individual history. It is the result of a complex process that "is not reducible to a method (or even several methods) of thinking; it is also a way of perceiving."[236] This way of perceiving is difficult to make visible, as are the central qualities of skilled caring involved in nursing work. Indeed, another problem with evidence is related to the difficulty of making visible and measurable much of the caring work that nurses perform.

With the new health reforms, however, there is a risk that selected evidence will become a substitute for judgement, or at least a way of significantly limiting judgement. Such evidence may be treated as truth, as a formula that allows managers to make decisions about care. In new quality assurance schemes, accountability is really about counting, about defining responsibility in numerical and financial terms. And quality is assumed to flow inevitably from a system with accountability mechanisms.

Health reform strategies thus often define accountability, as well as appropriate care, in terms of evidence based on what is or can be counted. As US management experts Donald Berwick, Blanton Godfrey and Jane Roessner explain in *Curing Health Care*, "It is a characteristic of quality management to invest heavily in the design and deployment of measurement. The agenda for measurement is extensive."[237] "If you can't measure it, you can't manage it"[238] is a fundamental principle in the new health care management philosophy. By definition, what counts is what can be counted. As *Closer to Home* puts it, health outcomes "must be defined, measurable, subject to analysis and be able to be independently evaluated." Independent evaluation often means management evaluation and evaluation through measurement in numerical terms.

This approach, then, brings together particular kinds of evidence from medicine and from management, often making cost and control both the primary concerns and the primary measures of success. The assumption is that it is possible to determine technically how to get the right people treated in the right way for the right amount of time by the right people by getting the right statistical data and using them to manage diagnoses, treatment and care.

The purpose of this evidence-based decision-making is to standardize care so that it can be readily managed in ways that reduce costs. In the process, judgements by providers may be limited through increasingly strict guidelines for both diagnosis and treatment. For doctors, there is evidence-based medicine, defined as treatment "based on scientific research rather than tradition or habit"[239] and practice guidelines. Combined with population and other data, this evidence might be used for utilization reviews by management in ways that restrict the professional choices of providers and the personal choices of patients. Evidence from population health and from utilization reviews also could be used to predetermine the amount paid per patient in each region, clinic or institution.

For nurses, care paths are "the more specifically tailored cousin of practice guidelines."[240] Like practice guidelines, care paths can set out strict guidelines for what nurses can do according to the diagnostic category of their patients. These paths can even substitute for the nursing care plans nurses have long developed, which were based on evidence, experience and individual patients. At the same time, care work may be divided into task bytes that can be fed into a computer and infinitely manipulated by management to establish rigid parameters for the time it takes to complete particular care tasks. The data are developed to determine how people should be treated, how long they should be treated and how many people, with what qualifications, should treat them. Although the purpose is to make care based more on evidence than on individual judgment while decreasing costs, there is very little scientific evidence to support the claim that these managerial approaches improve either quality or accountability more broadly defined.[241]

Quality Care

The nurses interviewed for this study want quality care for their patients and recognize that there is always room for improvement, especially in such rapidly changing times. They support the notion of basing decision-making on evidence. Indeed, their education has led them to value scientific evidence highly and to support the careful coordination of care. Their experience has taught them that evidence also comes from actually doing the work, from providing care on a daily basis to individual patients. In their view, case management and nursing plans combine these two kinds of evidence. Although the nurses point out that there have always been protocols for some kinds of care and guidelines to follow in other areas of care provision, more accountability based on sound evidence could be useful.

These nurses favour such guidelines not only because nurses continue to recognize the importance of evidence as a basis for care, but also because they know there has been some inappropriate care in the past. They also know that there has been abuse encouraged by financial incentives to provide as much treatment as possible rather than what is needed for good care. But they see fundamental problems with the way the guidelines are being developed and implemented under the current pressure to cut costs and the emphasis on management evidence over nursing evidence. They also see a basic contradiction between the rush towards standardization and the recognition of both the art involved in providing care and individual differences among patients.

Nursing, they explain, is at the core of health care.

> At 3:00 in the morning when everybody's tucked in bed, the social workers go home, the psychologists go home, and the managers go home, and the dietitians go home and the housekeeping staff go home, the doctors go home. When the whole world goes home from 8:00 in the evening till 8:00 the next morning, there's only a registered nurse between you and death. And that's all there is to it. For half the day, half of 24 hours in a hospital everywhere in BC. Everywhere, Canada, it's only a registered nurse.

It is not simply a matter of nurses being the only people there. Their care is critical to patient health; in other words, critical to the quality of care. On this, the evidence is mounting. Most of the relevant research has been carried out in the United States, but it indicates that the RN/patient ratio makes a difference. There are better health outcomes and survival rates where there are more registered nurses.[242] Equally important, the evidence suggests that there are better outcomes when nurses are allowed to use their judgement and follow professional standards.[243] Yet nurses are less and less able to provide the kind of care, based on their training, experience and professional commitment, that the evidence suggests leads is the best quality care.

Less Time to Care; Less Time to Rest

One factor preventing quality care is the reduction in the time available for care. Managerial strategies are constantly reducing the time available to provide what nurses' experience tells them is appropriate care, in spite of their protests.

> This is what I'm telling to management, who want us to hurry up and we have no time: "You're nursing in the '70s. You have no time to rub a back now. For God's sake, come up to the '90s." When I'm rubbing that patient's back I'm talking to him, I'm looking at his skin, I'm evaluating him, I'm listening to his mentation and getting to know him. How can you ever get to know someone, even if it takes you three

minutes, how can you ever get to know these people? They don't need to be training the type of people that traditionally go into nursing now, the caring, the feeling, the wanting-to-help person. You need to–if this is the way nursing's going–then you need to train people who are mathematicians or task oriented. You get it done and you bugger off, or you don't spend the time. Oh, I don't know. I just think, I have nursed now since 1961. I went to training in January of '61 and I've loved it and I love nursing, but this time I am thinking I would leave now if you could pay me enough money to get out. And that's a terrible thing to say because I have no time to love it any more. You hit that ward at a run, and you're always having to say to people, "I haven't got time to do that, I'm sorry sir." and it's a horrible way to nurse.

Time available is further reduced by the increasing acuity level of patients in care and by new strategies such as day surgery and out-patient services. Although the management language is one of patient-focused care, the speed at which people are processed through the system combined with the heavy patient load make it impossible for nurses to focus on people rather than on tasks and body parts. The nurses all agreed with the individual who said, "Sometimes I'm so busy with body parts that I really almost forget and lose track of what the body parts are connected to, you know." Another went on to say that

You don't ever really have a history on the person now. The patient doesn't come in the night before their surgery. You don't have a chance to read over that chart before they go to the OR. You just get this person back from the OR having had an anesthetic and they react whatever way they do. And you think, "where are they coming from?" So you don't know the person as a person, talk to them…even that time before where they might have been anxious, you would have seen that anxiety. You don't have a chance to make some kind of a bond with them so that when they come back, you're not a stranger to them.

With new managerial strategies, a major part of the problem is that "time periods are so short and so tight" and the only patients allowed to stay in hospital require a lot of care. Many of those who in the past received care in the hospital have now been shifted to long-term care facilities, creating similar problems for nurses who work there. Neither funding nor "care hours for the resident in the bed" have changed since reforms began, but the care each resident in a long-term care facility requires has increased enormously. "When I started there in 1974 we were funded for two and a half hours of care a day. We're still funded for two and a half hours of care a day. And that is completely insane." Similarly, more acutely sick and injured patients are being sent home from hospital, without an appropriate increase in community nursing care time.

Nursing staffs have not been increased to cover the increase in care requirements, in part because management defines care time only in terms of tasks that can be measured easily, and then sets out to reduce that time as much as possible by speeding up the work. Yet nurses see care as critical to quality, as well as to nursing work. As one nurse put it,

> I think for me nursing is caring. And I think that if you come into the hospital and you feel like I care about what happens to you [it has] just such a tremendous effect on how quickly you'll get better or how you'll feel about your treatment. So for me that's what nursing is. I mean, you can talk about the tasks and the technical stuff but really I think that that is one of the main things—if you feel like you've been taken care of, like someone cares about you.

This care is not simply a matter of commitment; it is an integral part of the work that cannot be measured easily. Caring significantly adds to the complexity of each task, and thus to the time required. Management systems, however, seldom take this kind of care time into account when calculating how many nurses are required per patient and per shift.

The speed-up created by the quick processing of patients and the extra labour required for each patient makes it less and less possible for nurses to provide the care their experience and training tell them is central to quality and to appropriate health outcomes. Nurses have responded to this speed-up by working harder and longer, often without pay for their extra hours and without the rest needed to perform well on the job. They talked about this extraordinary effort in interview after interview.

> Well, it's so busy. I guess we just work harder. And you hear everyone saying that. The nurses have not yet let the patients slide. We're injuring ourselves. And the burn out, and the stress leaves now, because people are just…they don't want to let go of any of that. I hear the nurses [in the] uro-gyne ward, and I remember hearing them say, "We stay overtime now because we're not prepared to give up that care," and "We don't charge management because they don't want us to do that." They don't want us to spend time with the patients any more. And I don't mean just time talking. I mean time changing a dressing that really should be changed. I mean, yes, it could wait

probably another four hours, but it's mucky, and it's really uncomfortable for the patient, and it should be changed. But management would say, "If it could be done in the next shift, if it can be left for the next shift, then leave it." What they don't understand is the next shift have enough to do, they don't want to be picking up what you haven't been able to do.

The time problem has been further exacerbated by restructuring. Through the amalgamation of services, management seeks to streamline processing and eliminate any time or service defined as waste. The time that once came with variations resulting from responses to individual patient needs and demands for specific services is rapidly disappearing. Indeed, that is one purpose of amalgamation.

Nurses were exhausted before we restructured and looked at managed care. Now it's even worse because there's this perception that we're...in a widget factory and we've got to keep on moving all the time. If nurses aren't allowed down time and rest time and a little bit of respite while they're at work, they can't function. But you can't tell that to the people who want to bring in managed care.

This extraordinary effort is one of the reasons nurses distrust the limited evidence that management produces on the effectiveness of its strategies. The statistics show only the hours the nurses are paid to work, not the extra time they put in during and after their recorded hours or the extra effort that is put out at great individual cost.

Less Time to Learn; Less Time to Teach

A second factor preventing quality care is the failure to provide the conditions that allow nurses to learn about how to offer appropriate care. Those we interviewed made clear that nursing is not something that is learned once during formal education. It is an on-going process, a never-ending learning period that happens as much on the job as it does in formal sessions, whether at a post-secondary institution or as an in-service event at a hospital. Although many nurses made this point, one provided a particularly clear explanation of how nurses learn on the job.

Nursing, learning nursing, is a 24-hour job, like child care. Like you know when you have a child the learning comes from the constant presence of the child and your relationship with the child. And nursing, learning nursing is the same thing. Like seeing a patient in the morning, lunch time, supper time, you know. Come on shift the next day and they're in their night time mode. So you know it's a process of being with somebody, not just the jobs you do to somebody.

Shortened patient stays, day surgery that rushes people through, out-patient clinics and task-oriented means of measuring care allow little time for this kind of learning. Nurses report that they have no time to teach the student nurses and no time to teach the casual, part-time and floating nurses allocated to their areas.

The problem of having no time to teach and learn is further exacerbated by the new methods that are constantly introduced, often without appropriate preparation for the nurses. A new procedure for dealing with fetal death was just one example among many the nurses offered. A medication begins the process of delivering the fetus. A doctor specializes in this method, but the nurses have not been taught how to deal with what happens next.

The patients just take this orally and then they'll start to abort the baby. And this was all very fine. But they haven't got the protocol in place yet to tell us exactly what steps we're supposed to do. Plus the urology nurses have never done this before and we're half the staff on the floor. And I thought, "This is good. So we have ladies coming in and aborting their babies and no one's taught us anything." Is this a transfer of function? Is this actually a nurse's job to do this or not? And we don't know. And I've gone to the clinical teacher to say, "We need to get trained on this because we've been here now since the beginning of June and you said as soon as those things were in place you would tell us exactly how to do it."

So you just pray every time you go to work there's a gyne nurse on that floor with you for your shift. Because otherwise, well, I guess you'd just have to call the gynecologist on call and hope he'll come and help you with whatever you're dealing with 'cause you don't know what you're doing. No one's taught you yet.

It is not only new procedures and new technology that require means and opportunities for continuous learning, it is also the new demands created by the rapid managerial and structural changes underway. Amalgamation brings together in a single area patients with very different problems. As a result, nurses much more frequently face unfamiliar treatments and technology.

And we see that in the recovery room, because we look after patients from a wide variety…especially with all this transition. The wards that are amalgamated, they all phone up and ask, "Well, do you know about this or whatever?" And we do really try and go down and give them a hand. You don't have enough clinical experts around even, you know, they don't necessarily have the nurses on the ward and I don't feel they probably have enough clinical resource nurses always.

In spite of these massive changes, many of these nurses say they "don't have any more in-service education than we had three and a half years ago or five or eight years ago." Nurses provided example after example of how this failure to train reduces the quality of care.

I cannot believe how they don't help anybody with the skills, clinical skills. Listen to this one. I was on nights last week. I couldn't believe it. I was so tired, I was so busy, and I get a phone call at 6:30 in the morning, desperate, from a girl from the short stay. The patient is supposed to be doing his own self-catheterization but he can't get it in. And there's no orderly on in emerg until 7:30 in the morning and the man's desperate. "Could I come up?" And I'm thinking, "Oh geez. The last thing I feel like doing is going up and helping this person right now." I did. And she was doing so many things wrong and I thought, "It's not my job to be telling her…" I'm going to talk to the clinical teacher when I go back this week to say, "These guys were out in left field. They didn't know what they were doing." I mean these are basic skills that some RNs don't have now.

It seems to these nurses that this is a long way from ensuring the right care by the right person at the right time.

This concern about learning among new nurses was expressed frequently by the nurses with many years of experience. The new environment does more than limit learning time for new nurses. It teaches them a very different kind of nursing. The experienced nurses fear that with no time to care, nurses will learn only specific tasks, and these tasks will be about specific body parts rather than about whole people in need. The older nurses have seen their own possibilities for providing nursing care disappear already.

I mean, when I trained it was totally different from what I ended up nursing in the hospital. And that's why I got out of the hospital and into the community. Because I couldn't [do that kind of nursing]. I was losing that human kind of touch and being able to hold someone's hand and give them that TLC that they need when they're going through a rough time, which you can't do 'cause you're running doing all the tasks. Or phoning doctors and getting orders. So that's why I went into the community…and I'm very happy in the community. I mean, I just couldn't imagine going back into the hospital. But now the community is being threatened in sort of the same way in that they want us to be slotting people into [categories].

The more experienced nurses also worry that even many of the tasks that have traditionally been central to quality caring in nursing, such as foot care and back rubs, will no longer be learned by nurses squeezed for time, pressured to get the minimum done and to focus on the most technical tasks. Indeed, some of the young nurses we interviewed had no experience doing this kind of caring work and some of them could not understand why foot care or back rubs should be done.

New ways of managing and organizing further reduce the possibilities for the continuous learning that is so critical to appropriate care. Team nursing, for example, has been eliminated in many areas in favour of primary care nursing, in which each nurse is assigned a set of patients rather than a set of broad tasks, such as administering medications. The nurses who supervise are now trained to play primarily a management role, rather than a teaching one. The clinical nurses who are supposed to play a teaching role are seldom there when they are needed and are spread too thinly among the new amalgamated areas. More than one nurse

much preferred team nursing…It's OK with primary-care nursing if you've got the right amount of nurses and your ward, your patients, are pretty equally balanced. But if you end up with four of your five patients critical or really ill, you're run off your feet. And I liked it when you had a team leader and a med nurse and then you had your LPNs [licensed practical nurses] helping out. And I think that the spirit and the ward cohesiveness was much better 'cause you were working as a team and you helped each other…But now, of course, if you're in primary nursing, there isn't the communication.

Less Recognition of the Skills Involved; Less Attention to the Evidence

A third factor these nurses see preventing quality care is the failure to recognize nursing skills and their importance in providing appropriate care. The nurses see evidence of this failure in a variety of new managerial strategies. One kind of evidence can be found in the new "charting by exception" means of recording nurses' assessments of patient conditions. The nurses call it "tick charting." These nurses have learned to write down any details they think are important after they have assessed a patient, based on their experience, training and knowledge of the individual patient. In this new system, "They don't want to know anything unless it's terribly wrong." This method of recording contradicts the nurses' training. As one nurse put it, "We're finding it most frustrating because we're so used to listening to chests, and when you listen to someone's lung sounds you want to document that, you know." But the issue for these nurses is not simply about resisting a new practice merely because it differs from the old one or because it requires learning something else. It is about quality of care and a recognition of the skills involved in that care.

Nurses' experience tells them that all patients are different, and thus all patients are in some ways exceptions. Each requires individual, experienced assessment to determine what is an aberration for that patient. Charting by exception is based on the opposite assumption: that most patients are the same and only aberrations from a standard patient are to be noted. One nurse's explanation of how the system works made their objections clear.

> You sign in a little square box because on Day 3 post op they should have their IV out. So if their IV isn't out, you put a circle around the box and then you have to go to the charting nurse as to why that's a variance of what's expected. By Day 5 at 11:00 a.m. they've gone home...And there's always a difference. But they're saying, "Well on Day 1, we expect them to sound a bit wet. On Day 2 they should be a bit drier. But I mean that varies so much from person to person...Oh, you have to be pretty sick for us to write anything about you now.

> It's a sheet. OK, we have a normal chart, the old chart, binder thing. And you do have the lined patient progress, if you choose. But they don't really want you to use that, righ? They want you to use this sheet which you open out to this size, and it's Day 1 and those are the expected outcomes. And you just put your initial. You don't even sign. You sign at the bottom of the sheet that you, [Jane Doe] 7:30 to 3:30, so you just see my squiggle in the box if everything's gone normally. And if I look down there and the chest tubes are supposed to be out, and they're not, then you'll see a circle around it and you have to go to the narrative charting and read why they aren't out. Too much drainage, or...at least we're still taping report, but we're going away from that, too. It's actually going to be a sheet of paper that you pass to the next

shift with your ticks on it, and that'll be your report. There's no overlap and no wasting time with reports, except in the critical-care areas. They get 15 minutes still. But we had to go to arbitration for that. 'Cause they wanted all areas to get rid of the overlap.

Such charting encourages only a minimal assessment and, the nurses fear, could lead to nurses missing important signs in patients. It will also limit nurses' capacity to pass on knowledge about less measurable signs, and this knowledge can be critical to care.

It's scary. I think it's scary…There's soon to be no "I feel like he's depressed" or "I think that this family dynamic," or "I'm not too sure about the look of that leg." Because how do you document that [with ticks]? You know, "Keep an eye on his leg 'cause it just looks a little funny to me." A lot of nursing is gut feelings. And most of it, you're dead right. But unless you can pass that on to the next shift, things are going to be missed or happen.

Another kind of evidence that indicates this failure to recognize the skills involved in nursing work can be found in the attempts to divide nursing work up into a set of specific tasks. Once the tasks are defined, then the tasks are divided up into jobs that can be done by people with less training and thus, it is assumed, receiving lower pay. A hospital nurse summed up this strategy succinctly:

As we become task oriented, then our managers, our employers, give the tasks away. So if you break up nursing into a task then you break up what we do as a profession. So you can't–we're trying not to have our profession be slotted up into little compartments that can be given away and they can say, "Well, one and two we can actually get somebody cheaper to do." There's all these asinine studies that say that 70 per cent of what a registered nurse does is a waste of time. All this down time all the time.

The problem is not merely that RNs would lose some of their work to others. It is also that many of these tasks cannot easily be isolated and parcelled out without losing critical aspects of care. The complex relation-ships among tasks, and the knowledge that comes with their interrelationship, will be lost, often to the detriment of patient care and to the long-term costs of the system. Nurses offered example after example to illustrate the impor-tance of skilled nursing in assuring quality care.

One such example concerned a patient sent home shortly after surgery. Care was provided, but it was care by a home care aide, without input from an RN. While it may seem appropriate to have home care workers with little formal medical training do the cooking, cleaning, toileting, feeding and other care services for elderly people who do not require high-tech care, there is a real danger that such providers will miss important signals about health problems.

The only trouble is they don't pick up the variables. It happened in home care actually. One of our RNs had a friend who'd had a hip replacement. And she was going to visit her every day. Now this friend also had a home care worker coming in and helping. She was an elderly woman. And she was wearing slacks all the time. And one time [the RN] went when she was in a nightie. [The RN] looked at her and said, "How does your leg feel? It looks very swollen." And she said, "It's really been sore, like down here...But my little home worker's been working so hard. She's got the A5-35 and she's rubbing it like mad, massaging it." And [the RN] said, "I think you better go and see your physician tomorrow." Of course she was admitted with deep vein thrombosis. But the health care provider that she had didn't have a clue. Didn't even twig. But as soon as an RN–I mean, if you've had surgery you're looking for deep vein thrombosis if people are having leg pain, right? But this woman possibly would have died.

Another example concerned much more high-tech intervention in the hospital, where many of the tasks that were formerly reserved for registered nurses are being transferred to nurses with fewer years of formal training, and less pay.

There's all kinds of that happening. They decided to allow practical nurses in my region, in my facility, to feed people and give medications to patients through what they call a G tube, which is a catheter. And it's got a balloon and it's stuck into somebody's stomach. OK. So the practical nurse comes out one day and she's been taught how to do it. She's passed the course, and she says to the RN, "I can't get the medication to go down." So the RN says, "Let me go in and have a look at it and see what's happening." Sure enough they can't get it down. So the RN says, "In this instance what we do is we take it back, a syringe, and we pull the water out of the balloon to see whether the balloon is actually occluding the opening." So they stick in the syringe and they pull out almost 60 cc of medication within the balloon. If that had eventually ruptured, the patient would have had all this medication in their system.

Similar problems can arise in surgical wards, where more and more tasks are no longer the exclusive preserve of the RNs.

They decided in my facility that on surgical floors the RNs were getting busy, practical nurses could remove intravenous. So they said, "If a doctor comes along and writes an order you can remove the intravenous." So the practical nurse sees "remove intravenous from patient so-and-so. I know that patient. That's my patient." So she ticks off. She goes down the hall, she looks at the patient, says, "The doctor says your IV can come out." And the patient says, "Oh great, that's great. I can get up and go outside for a cigarette." So she comes in and she takes out the intravenous and she says to the RN who she's team leading with, "I just took out the intravenous on Mr. So-and-So." The RN says, "You did what?" "Well, the doctor wrote the order." Well, you don't follow an order just because a doctor wrote it. You have to assess whether it's right. And most LPNs can't. They're so concrete thinking, and their training is task oriented, whereas an RN has to be more comprehensive in her work or his work or whatever. So anyway she says, "That patient had an output last night of 120 cc's. They're dehydrated. That patient does not have bowel sounds yet. You had no business taking that IV out, that intravenous out. We have to hydrate that patient. Not only that, I have one more antibiotic to give intravenously, but because you don't give meds on this floor and I do, you didn't know that. So not assessing those three external factors, you just went in and removed a vein, a patient's IV, an IV from a patient's vein. You performed a task on a vein. I, as the RN, am looking after that whole person and I know exactly what's impacting on that person today."

A nurse doesn't stop an intravenous, she doesn't stop the medication if the doctor tells her to. That's what people don't understand. In society we have safeguards set up in our hospitals that a registered nurse is your last line. And if a registered nurse thinks you need an IV, you get an IV. If a registered nurse thinks you need more antibiotics she's going to be on the phone for that. If she thinks you need more narcotics she's going to be on the phone.

Most nurses were quick to point out that they are not blaming the practical nurses or the home care workers for taking on the tasks of RNs. Nor are they dismissing the work of these other providers as unskilled. Moreover, they recognize that many of the LPNs and home care workers have developed important skills that complement and supplement those of RNs. But in many cases, those trained to do the specific care tasks do not have enough formal training to know what they do not know. "And you only find out because they made the mistake." In some cases, the other providers have picked up the necessary knowledge on the job, as they work in teams. But the system cannot be designed on the assumption that these skills have been acquired by these other providers.

Instead of blaming other providers for this transfer of tasks, the majority of these nurses see the problem mainly as a managerial one. Increasingly, managers trained in managing rather than in nursing fail to understand the skilled nature of the work and focus on short-term cost savings, often implementing strategies from other sectors that do not work in health care. Many of the nurses we interviewed are strongly committed to retaining the full range of nursing tasks because they see such tasks as integral to nursing work.

> Our managers are saying, or both our managers, the old one and the new one, "Come on...there's room for practicals in here. They could make your beds for you." And I say, "There's room for practicals but as an adjunct for RNs." They could help me make the bed. I still want to make the bed because I've got my patient sitting in the chair and I'm asking him, "So, when you go home how many pounds are you supposed to be lifting? And what should you be avoiding? And what are you watching for? What is a sign, what would make you go back to your doctor?" I'm talking to the patient and assessing the patient's teaching needs and everything while I'm making his bed, while I'm washing his back, while I'm wiping his bum.

Nurses see nursing as the core of health care, and they see the patient contact that comes with performing the full range of tasks as critical in allowing them to provide the skilled aspects of their work. They cannot, for example, easily do the skilled task of assessing the patient unless they are also bathing the patient. Or at least, if they do separate the tasks of assessing and bathing, then the nurses are wasting time because they are not doing two tasks at once, something managers seek to avoid. Equally important, by eliminating the bath, nurses are eliminating an important opportunity to provide care while doing the assessment. As one nurse with years of experience put it,

> [Patients] don't go there for medical care. They go mainly for nursing

care. That's why hospitals were started up. They were started up by the nuns and everything for nursing care. OK? Part of that nursing care is contact with the patient, a lot of contact. And that means when a registered nurse does a bed bath, that supposedly very menial chore, that nurse is doing head to toe assessment, whether that person's cognitive functioning is there, whether–I mean, nurses just are constantly scanning. We find out more about weird bruises on somebody's back that don't make sense, about, you know, we can find out more by spending time with the patient. And because the patients trust us, we do still have that credibility with the public and that trust.

He wants to know that when he goes into the hospital that some [untrained person] isn't going to come and give him a bed bath and not understand what the two bruises on his back mean or, you know, some other physical symptom which a nurse will say, "This guy's got two of them. This guy fell last night. He's bleeding around the area of his kidneys." You know. "His urine's dark." And a nurse just automatically puts that all together.

The less-experienced nurses we interviewed were less committed to keeping the bathing work. The issue became a matter of debate in several interviews. The older nurses were convinced that this lack of concern about bathing reflected the new work structure, which no longer allows nurses to learn to provide care.

Although there were debates among the nurses about the full range of nursing tasks and about what could be done by others, all of the nurses we interviewed were concerned about the process of nursing being defined as a set of specific tasks that could be individually assigned to different kinds of workers. They were not, however, convinced that this meant nursing work was being de-skilled in the sense that it no longer required important skills. Indeed, they saw the new managerial strategies as increasing the demands for skills among all workers, although often without the provision of the required training.

About the breaking down of the tasks, right, because then you can hand it over to anybody...OK. Here's what I say to that. We live in times where the patient acuity has gone sky-high for a couple of reasons. We don't keep people in very long. You have to be very sick, critically sick to stay in a hospital now. So I don't think that any profession will look at itself and say we're de-skilling, you know, because the acuity is going to continue to rise. Physicians are going to see sicker and sicker and sicker people. Nurses are going to have to look after sicker and sicker people. LPNs are going to have to look after sicker and sicker people. I mean, that acuity is driving, is a big driving force.

In other words, RNs will certainly not lack complicated things to do, nor will the LPNs or home care aides. But the nurses see critical skills–registered nursing skills that the evidence suggests are essential to quality care–disappearing in the process of task definition and task transfer.

Accountability

Accountability as Counting: A Statistical Basis for Care

For nurses, closely related to the failure of managers to recognize nursing skills is the problem with attempts to measure what nurses do and standardize both the care process and nursing time.

Managers and consultants of various kinds from outside the institutions have become increasingly important in developing reform strategies. Although the nurses recognize that managerial and academic skills can be valuable, managers without experience in nursing too often do not see the complex relationship among tasks. Their academic or managerial training could even prevent them from seeing how apparently simple tasks involve quite skilled aspects when done in the context of health care work. In addition, they could miss the most critical components of care in their attempts to eliminate what their management training has led them to define as waste. The nurses we interviewed have had direct experience with attempts to quantify their work. Here is one experience with a consultant conducting a study designed to determine the time and skill involved in weighing patients.

And she says, "Well I just take temperatures and blood pressures and I write them down on this thing and I ask them how old they are." You know, like how difficult is that? So the person that was running this thing, the PhD lady, said, "Why would we have a registered nurse?" And I said, "because if I put that child on a weigh scale and weigh them, I check that child's spine, I check that child for bruises, I check that child's muscular development, I check that child's hair, I check that child's ears. I check a lot more on that child and I can scan that, in 15 seconds I can know more about that child by looking than this person who can just take a temperature and stuff like that and write it down." I said, "I know the significance of…vital signs."

The nurses had great difficulty convincing the consultant that weighing patients involves much more than reading a scale and that the complex task takes more time than simply reading and writing down information and requires more skill than is required to read a digit. In fact, the actual weighing is often a minor part of an assessment process that involves a broad range of knowledge about health and care.

At the same time that outside consultants are hired to determine systems for counting care work, the nurses inside the system report being excluded from the counting process, in spite of their considerable expertise. To these nurses, their exclusion suggests that good evidence collected in order to ensure quality care is not the main objective. In one institution,

> There's about 20 people on this task force and I looked at it very quickly and I said to our VP, "You know this absolutely amazes me. You're talking about a documentation task force. You're talking about the work that the bedside nurse is going to be doing." And I said, "You don't have one nurse on this. One bedside nurse. You don't have one person on this committee who is actually going to be doing the work at the end of the day." They're all managers and, you know, clinical nurse specialists and all these people who haven't seen a dirty bottle in their lives or at least for many years.

The nurses report that their managers are just beginning to use this kind of research as a basis for determining how much nursing time is required for various tasks, how long patients need for each treatment, and how many beds are necessary.

> If you come in for a gall bladder and we're doing a laparoscopy you really only need to stay in for X number of hours and so we're going to start moving the patients a lot quicker and so we'll free up all these beds, right? So we don't need all those beds.

Yet these nurses do not think that the available statistics can provide reliable information on what care is necessary for individual patients. One reason for their scepticism is that the assessment of nursing time required seems to be inadequate and so does the assessment of variability among patients; evidence that provides the basis for staffing decisions seems to underestimate both. This is already evident in the constant need to work overtime and to call in casually employed nurses. Inadequate staffing has a profound impact on the quality of care nurses can provide, and on the stress levels nurses experience.

It is also inefficient. Nurses spend far too much time seeking extra help when it is required. They report that they "have to phone and beg and borrow and kiss boots and prove all kinds of things before they'll let us have help. Well, by then your emergency's done" and nurses have wasted valuable nursing time trying to get help. "What this management nowadays don't seem to realize 'is that when you're going through a crisis on your ward, the last thing you have time for is to pick up the phone and try and get help." Nurses are regularly "calling workload," which "means that there's not enough staff to look after the patients."

> You have a ward and you have 40 patients on it. And during the day time you have one registered nurse and one practical nurse for ten patients, OK? And that's what you're [assigned]. Your acuity shoots sky-high for some reason. And you consistently need to have an extra RN for at least four hours every single day. Over time that is the position that should be there. That shouldn't be somebody that you call. That should be a regular position and filled by somebody... It goes from the nurse to the manager.

This understaffing happens in spite of evidence indicating that there is a constant demand and a regular need for more nurses.

> The nurses have consistently gone to the manager over a period of time, for instance, and said, "We need an extra person on evenings. We can't cope because of this, this and this. And look at all your overtime stats." And so the manager will then say, "Well OK, we'll play it by ear. We'll do it by workload and I'll book someone in. What days do you think you're busiest?" And we'll book someone in regularly and see if that lowers it. But then if a patient dies, they'll cancel that workload person.

Some of the evidence on which decisions on staffing are based may be unreliable for other reasons. For example, one institution used a system called Medicus to measure staffing needs. The nurses claimed that the system was simply adjusted to meet management goals in ways that ignored the evidence. According to one nurse, "You have to write it in pencil. The manager takes it off and rubs it all out and writes in what she wants. And it is useless anyway."

When the evidence on nursing shortages mounts, or is taken seriously, the nurses fear that the solution will not be to hire more registered nurses on a regular basis. Instead, because these measurement tools fail to recognize the skilled nature of the work and because the focus is on cost saving rather than on quality care, the solution could well be to hire less knowledgeable or untrained helpers.

The nurses are just as concerned about the evidence, or lack thereof, for care pathways that determine the length of stay for patients. In the case of early discharge, they see little indication that evidence is collected on the cost or quality impact of the strategy. Nurses in every interview questioned whether the data were even being collected.

> I think even in acute care there's some question, in my mind anyway, as to whether or not all this rapid out-the-door business as soon as you can breathe twice and that kind of thing is actually cost efficient either, because there have been so far no consistent follow-up studies to show how many readmissions there are and how many infections there are that require treatment by antibiotics and by whatever under the sun. I think there's an early one out on the lower mainland to do with readmissions of new baby and moms from rapid discharge after delivery and this kind of thing, but there have been no real studies done so far to say that sending people home when they can breathe twice straight in a line is cost efficient, because we don't know how many of them end up either back in again or have complications that they wouldn't have had if they'd stayed in a little longer. You know. We don't know that. We're assuming or some bean counters are assuming that this is more efficient because we can show right here today this person has gone home sooner.

Some of the evidence that is collected hides the actual costs and actual patient distress. For one thing, it does not calculate the unpaid overtime nurses put in to ensure that their patients do not suffer. For another, the method for collecting the data might camouflage what the actual costs are.

For example, in one facility, "We only have one chart per patient. It's assumed that our people will come back." And when they come back, "Because it's an out-patient facility their chart is available and it's used for each admission." Thus, if patients come back to the out-patient facility because they have complications from early discharge that mean they require more care, "they're not really called admissions. They're follow-up." As a result, the data do not capture the extra costs from the early discharge strategy. Instead, the statistics inaccurately suggest that it is all part of one care package.

When patients do not return to the hospital, this does not necessarily mean that early discharge was an effective and efficient approach. The costs of suffering and of extra care may be borne entirely by the individual and thus remain invisible in the data. As one nurse put it,

> I would say that of those ten patients [discharged early], two might be going to facilities and the rest are going home. And…I think one of the statistics that'll never show up is the people who are sent home and are told that they are OK, they are going to cope there until they are in real trouble. So statistically it still looks good. I mean, I'm sure there are some people who go home and struggle for two weeks that the health care system will never know about.

Similarly, patients who experience complications at home add costs to the system. But the budget is different, and the costs of early discharge are absorbed into that other budget and thus disappear from the hospital accounts. A community care nurse explained how this works:

> If they come to me, 'cause I'm in the continuing-care environment as opposed to extended-care environment, I can get added care for them and that never gets counted as a cost for that surgery. They come back to us early, we get added care, it's paid for from [a specific] Health Region. And that statistic never shows up.

Even if the evidence is collected, however, these nurses fear that the criteria for success will be strictly financial. They fear that any reduction in beds will be cheaper and there will be much less importance attached to the few people whose health suffers as a result of this strategy. The nurses report that they "see the bounce back," the return of patients discharged too early from care. However, readmitting these patients might be less expensive for the hospital than keeping more people longer. Concerned about the cost to patients in terms of health, a nurse was not convinced that the evidence would alter the practice because money could be saved.

> I really think that they will be able to prove statistically that the bounce back is not nearly as much as the discharge. They discharge roller-ball tuppers now in a 48-hour program…We would get the ones back that get into trouble, that start to bleed. And if they can discharge ten people a day from that program and they get one or two back, we're still ahead in the numbers and that's what they consider.

The nurses are also concerned that the measurement systems assume a curative model, assessing outcomes primarily in terms of who recovers or who leaves the institution. Care, however, is often required by people who will never be cured. As one nurse put it, few of the policy makers seem to be asking, "What is it that we're measuring to prove that we're doing a good job for the clients we're looking after?" In the case of elderly people, for example, "We're not trying to cure them. We're trying to make them have a quality of life in the last months or years that they're living. And it's really hard to measure. And it's not necessarily the most cost-effective" because the elderly cannot be swiftly moved through the system and declared fixed according to some measurable criteria. More, and different, methods for assessing quality are required if the full range of care needs are to be met.

The lack of reliable and appropriate evidence concerns these nurses, because dramatic changes are being made on the basis of existing evidence. They are equally concerned about defining evidence strictly in terms of what can be easily measured and manipulated statistically. The nurses have accumulated a great deal of evidence through their experience of caring for individuals, but this kind of evidence seems to be increasingly ignored in the new managerial strategies. Rather, the statistical evidence seems to be used to limit nurses' capacity to act on the basis of their experience. Equally important, the statistics too often ignore the important differences among patients, differences which are critical to quality care. Indeed, this seems to be the precise purpose of the statistics: to ignore differences and create single patterns for care.

Accountability through Patient Surveys

Patient satisfaction surveys are another method management employs to get statistical data intended to make nurses more accountable. Few patient surveys are currently used in British Columbia to transform or assess care, but they are being introduced. The nurses we interviewed are quite sceptical about evidence taken from patient satisfaction surveys, not because they reject patient input but rather because they do not think patients are in a position to judge many aspects of care. Health care is not like most other services in that health care services are usually undertaken out of necessity rather than choice. The services are often unavoidably unpleasant or even painful, leaving patients with little sense of satisfaction. At the same time, treatment that is inappropriate might be experienced as quite pleasant by the patient.

> I'm dead against surveys because I keep telling them you can have a survey and people can be very satisfied while they're eating cyanide. I mean, they don't know if they've had good or bad care and so patient satisfaction is beside the point. It's something we should care about because we should care about the service that we provide the public at the taxpayers' expense. Yes, let's care about it. But don't take that to

mean that we're providing quality care because sometimes, you know, there's a little pain involved with receiving quality health care. Sometimes kids cry when they get an injection. Sometimes it hurts. Sometimes it's ugly. Sometimes you don't hear the things you want to hear, and sometimes you have to take devastating news, like you have cancer. So patient satisfaction...is not a thermometer for the health care system.

These nurses are particularly concerned that patient satisfaction surveys could be used to measure overall quality. Many aspects of quality, they say, can be assessed only by professionals who understand the technical skills involved.

They don't measure the quality of health care, 'cause how can somebody who's not professional [assess quality]? That would be like saying to a lawyer, "I don't like that lawyer because he told me that I shouldn't take the witness stand." And that's the lawyer's advice. The lawyer's a professional. He knows what he's doing. Well, that person's dissatisfied with his lawyer but he doesn't realize that his lawyer's a pro. Well, we're the pros and I'm better able to tell you whether you had good care in the hospital.

This is not to suggest that patients cannot be consulted about the care they receive or appropriately evaluate some of the ways they are treated. Patients, for example, can assess how pleasant the nurse has been and that can be important to care. "If I smile a lot, you know, maybe that's nice" but even in the case of smiling, patients may not be aware of the conditions that make smiling difficult.

Equally important, if patient surveys are "the thermometer of quality," strategies to improve quality might focus on the wrong problems. Some nurses have already seen this happen. For example, a public relations team, in town to train people in another sector how to treat customers, was hired to help a hospital respond to complaints on satisfaction surveys.

They had these yokels come up to the hospital and teach us how to be a little friendlier because there were a lot of complaints about grumpy nurses. So they decided every single employee in the facility would have to spend six hours getting trained at employer expense...And I refused. I said, "You go ahead and discipline me. I used to be a flight attendant with Air Canada and I can stand there with the best of them and smile and say, 'Isn't this great? How are you doing, Mrs. Jones?'

I don't need your course." And in the end it cost $236,000–taken out of services–so that everybody could be taught to say when somebody says, "Nurse, I don't like the way I'm being treated." "Well, Mr. Jones…I think that what you think is legitimate. However, can I help you? What can I do, Mr. Jones?" Your pinky cut isn't an emergency. You're going to sit there and wait until we deal with this cardiac and if you don't like that you can write to [the manager].

The nurses are also concerned that patient satisfaction surveys can lead to the wrong solutions, especially when neither the patients nor the managers seem to understand the causes of the complaints. More than one nurse fears that the surveys will lead to their work being parcelled out to other providers rather than to the hiring of more RNs.

I have concern that these surveys, because the patients are observing that the nurses are very busy and yes, they are having to wait to have their bells answered at times, right? So I would be very afraid that on the survey, management would look at "The nurse couldn't come often enough" or something, and say, "Well, you were too busy making beds or giving bed pans so therefore the patients aren't getting the quality of attention that they want." So, we can replace you. Instead of getting more RNs, which is what they need, we'll just bring you in some helpers.

The use of patient satisfaction surveys is just part of the larger problem of reducing the assessment of quality to a matter of collecting data. Questions such as those on patient satisfaction surveys provide basic data that can then be transformed into formulas for care, in spite of the limitations in those data. One nurse summed up the issue in the following way:

I think you have to talk about what you mean by effective and efficient, because I mean, that's what you see: "You do the right thing at the right time at the right place," ad nauseam…Then you have this CQI [Continuous Quality Improvement] thing that says, "Ask the client what they want." And you wonder how does that effective, efficient doing the right thing at the right [time], from our perspective, marry up to the client outcome and what kind of satisfaction do they have when you do that? Because I don't think the two go together. From what I can see, effective, efficient, cost-effective, right care in the right place doesn't equal client satisfaction necessarily. And I think that piece of it's being left out. And we're just going down this road of effective efficiency without putting the piece in about quality. And I just find it's just so hard to quantify quality. Quality. Like we're trying to do it all the time at work.

In sum, these nurses think that patient surveys have only limited use. They cannot provide the basis for a full assessment of quality and can even lead to the wrong solutions.

Accountability through Participation and Information

New Directions promised both greater public participation, particularly through the provision of information, and more respect for care providers. Yet many of these nurses feel excluded from the decision-making processes, and these processes have a profound impact on their lives as workers and as citizens. More than one reported that "the government's made it really clear they don't want to hear from providers. They made that clear when they made the governing structures. Providers aren't on there." "We were not consulted" was a common refrain in the interviews. Even the information necessary for members of the public to participate was often difficult to gain access to.

Actually, we went to the freedom of information department or whatever and were told, "Well, just go back. They're supposed to give it to you. This is open stuff. This is public knowledge." We still never got it [the information]. I mean, you cannot go to the door of the finance office and bang on it and insist on things. So that's where the wall comes down. I can't believe that, I guess I have difficulty believing that the union reps and the stewards did not work really hard, but I think what probably happened is the same kind of thing that happened to us and that was you can work as hard as you like. You can go into those meetings asking for stuff, you know, over and over again, asking to be included in this process and they will not include you. And then what do you do, besides having a screaming fit. You know?

In some cases, nurses' efforts were successful and they were allowed to participate in at least parts of the decision-making process. One group explained that

We really fought hard…to have input and to have what we believe is our expertise heard for what would meet the needs of the residents best and [for] recognizing that we do have to live within a budget. I mean, we all pay our groceries, too, so most people know…you get X number of dollars and you have to do X number of things with it. But when push came to shove, despite our best efforts to obtain information so that we could have some input and say, "Look, let's look at it this way. Yes, we need to save $60,000 or $180,000" or whatever it was. Nurses can look at that realistically and still hopefully come out the other side with good-quality care for the patient or the resident.

In other words, they had to fight for what *New Directions* promised–respect and participation. But the victory was a hollow one. "We did not believe that we were listened to and I think I could speak for the nurses at my agency because I spoke with most of them over the last five months."
Some nurses were invited to participate in the decision-making.

We had representatives from each area attend these planning sessions. There was...so many phases in our restructuring and so there was a nurse [from another region] who went to Vancouver regularly to attend, along with the nurse manager. So she was a staff nurse, a grass roots nurse. And so initially we felt we had some representation.

Although these nurses reported being enthusiastic about this participation, they felt that the participation had little impact.

When the documents came out describing phase one, the planning phase and the implementation phase, what was said in the planning phase got changed in the implementation phase, so that what [the nurse participant] said was going on didn't end up happening.

Instead of meaningful participation, the nurses found that they were provided with such limited options that there were no choices to make.

There's a couple of techniques that are used in that kind of stuff. The technique is you hire a consultant to come in to interview everyone, and they either feed you four or five choices that you can choose and they're all satisfactory to the government structure or they manipulate you into agreeing to a path, and then they'll announce what they're going to do. It's already been decided. All this consultation is underneath the decision. And they say, "Oh, we consulted everyone. This is what they said." Well, they've manipulated you into–I remember participating as a head nurse and it was about the organizational structure of nursing within the [hospital] and they hired a nurse from [another province] to come and interview us all. Now some nurses didn't have any idea what they were even asked, but the choices they gave us were clear. They were all satisfactory to government. Didn't matter which one we chose, it was going to end up OK upstairs. I'm upstairs and I know the techniques from the other side. And I mean, so sure, you say you're consulted but you're consulted about what they want you to be saying.

Without necessary information, and with only limited, predetermined alternatives, these nurses feel there is little possibility for meaningful participation even when they are consulted.

Accountability through Flattened Hierarchies

Across Canada, managers have flattened hierarchies as a means of making individual employees more accountable. Middle management positions have disappeared and a new emphasis has been placed on teams that bear collective responsibility for their work. In health care, the majority of these middle managers were nurses who began their careers at the bedside. It is not surprising, then, that the most frequently eliminated position is that of head nurse. At the same time, unit managers and team leaders have become more common.

The nurses we interviewed held somewhat differing views about the removal of head nurses and the impact of that on accountability. Their views seemed to vary with the institutions and the particular way the new management strategy was implemented. One nurse, for example, attributed her positive experience to the specific characteristics of her area. "I would just like to [say] that in my experience, where I work, I don't think losing the head nurses has been that negative. I have felt that it has been empowering." She went on to suggest that "It has also made nurses quite accountable for what they're doing 'cause they can't just put it off to the head nurse." But she went on to add a qualifier to this claim. "I think that [it is] because of the kind of area we have. I mean, there are some leadership things that are...not there without the head nurse."

Coordination

Other nurses reported a range of problems arising from the elimination of the head nurse. Perhaps most obviously, the removal of head nurses can mean that there is no longer a single individual always there to be accountable for coordinating the work. The head nurse played a crucial coordinating role that linked the various aspects of nursing work and did so throughout the entire care period, at least according to a former head nurse who now does a different kind of management work.

I spent a lot of years being a head nurse and I think they had a role in the system. And I really do not agree with the elimination of head nurses. They're the glue that holds the unit together for nursing. And in about five years someone's going to come up with a wonderful idea that what we need as a coordinator of these units is a nurse. And I don't know what they'll call them, but I really think "head nurse" is a loss to the system because they coordinated; I mean, you're dealing with a seven-day-a-week, 24-hour care delivery system where people have to rotate through, and the glue was there and they've taken the glue away and they haven't replaced it with a nursing piece of glue. I could go with it if they had.

The head nurses have been replaced in some institutions by unit managers. But these supervisors are hired for only part of the day. "The unit managers are supposedly in charge from 7:15 until 3:15 in the afternoon." Equally important, each manager now covers a much larger area than the former head nurses. As a result, "They can be cross-site. They can have three or four units...they could be at [another campus] all day. So they're not in charge, really in charge." But the work of coordination and management tasks, such as replacing nurses calling in sick, does not disappear after 3:15 or when the unit manager is somewhere else. It still has to be done by the nurses who are there. "So nurses end up holding up the end of the stick without getting any financial reward for it."

Supervision
Those who still had at least a version of this kind of supervision reported that it was even more necessary in the face of cutbacks in the number of nurses and the employment of more people with fewer years of formal training.

I think in our setting we've gone to the team leader, which is essentially like a head nurse situation. We've had that in varying degrees and numbers for many years. And I'm pleased that at least part of it's continued to be supported by our administration because...our proportion of registered nurses to patients is so poor and because most of the care is given by care aides with four months' training. And the role of the head nurse...is really important in supervision and in continuity of care for these people because the registered nurses are spread so thin. And I would have real concern if we didn't have...that role in there because the RNs are...not paid to supervise and that's not what their role is. So we need that middle place.

For the majority of nurses who saw a need for such a paid supervisory role, it was critical that the role be filled by a registered nurse. Yet, in some cases, the elimination of head nurse can mean that the manager is a social worker or a therapist. Although these nurses say they respect the particular skills involved in social work and therapy, they do not think that people with such skills can manage nursing work. This is especially the case in these times of severe cutbacks in nursing staff because other providers often have to ask managers to help out with the direct care work or at least ask them for advice on how it should be done. It is very difficult for a non-nurse to fill this role. And as an increasing amount of the work gets done by those with only limited nursing training, the supervisory role of the registered nurse becomes even more critical to quality and accountability. A long-term care nurse offered her specific case to illustrate the problem.

> My actual job is going to change from looking after and being responsible for 35 patients to being responsible for 66...They've changed it so that instead of me being primarily responsible for 35 people with a med nurse working half with me and half with somebody else...there'll be a general duty nurse working with 35 people and a team leader working with two sets of 35, if you understand what I mean. Somewhere between 66 and 75 beds. So they've changed the rules, they've reduced the supervisory role in our facility for the second time in three and a half years. In our situation, because the care is primarily given by long-term care aides who have a four-month program, this impacts a lot...on patient care.

Even when the unit managers are all registered nurses, it is increasingly difficult for them to have the expertise necessary in their widely disparate units.

Mediation

The registered nurse in such a position acts as a buffer, mediating between the nurses who provide care and those who manage the system. "'Cause they're middle, they go both ways. The head nurse was also somewhat independent, allowing her to defend nurses on the basis of her own experience doing nursing work." The advantage of having a head nurse over having a unit manager was that a head nurse was in the nurses' union. The unit manager is not in the union, which

> makes a great difference [in terms of] of who your employer is and where your loyalties have to lie to keep your job. She was in the union

and they couldn't just say, "Sorry, you're gone tomorrow." Where [there was] a unit manager they could.

The movement from union membership means "It's a lot harder being an advocate" for nurses and nursing work. It is also much harder for managers to be advocates for nurses if they are not on site or if they have never had direct nursing experience, as is increasingly the case with the managers who remain.

In addition, as one nurse manager reported, there is the problem of communication. She had direct experience instituting the new management structure. "I flattened our organization when I first went into it and I just had nurses meet. And that worked in the little unit. The environment had 150 residents and it worked OK because we're three units and I could cope with that." The problems arose when a system that worked in a small area was applied to a large one, "when we moved into this new building that is just a nightmare architecturally."

I've got unit managers, two unit managers and myself and the nurses. And the unit managers' span of control is way too big for them to have any clinical expertise about care. So the clinical expertise is with the nurses. But if I want to communicate a change of clinical care delivery or the way we do things, I have to talk because I don't have a head nurse per unit. I have to talk to 15 different people on three different shifts to get the message across and I would like to be able to talk to one person who would be responsible for around-the-clock communication and then I'd only have to talk to six people to make that message clear. It's like that old game of password that you play when you're kids in that the message gets started and as it gets passed–and I'm really frustrated trying to communicate change or an operational thing or clinical way of doing things. Like we had a thing about advanced directives, the ERPs [emergency room physicians] didn't want a copy of our advanced directives. They wanted the original. Well, it took me two weeks to communicate what the nurses had to do, even with e-mail. But if I'd had head nurses I could have talked to six people all at once. We could have planned how we were going to do it and everyone would have known. So that piece of middle management is really important…It's the communication vehicle that you need to get good clinical care to the patient.

The new structures can not only limit communications; they can also increase the feeling of isolation and of total responsibility for care.

There's nobody to communicate with. Your nurse manager is a business manager in effect. There might be a clinical resource there but if she's split between two places you're not always going to see them. And if you don't have a background or experience in certain things, who do you ask? Who mentors you? There's no one, and that's why the nurses are feeling a little isolated. It's because they've got nobody to talk to.

In short, the system was less efficient with flattened hierarchies. Both the quality of care and the quality of information were reduced by the application of this strategy to areas where it was not appropriate.

"Most Responsible Nurses"
The new flattened hierarchies are intended to make teams, and individual nurses, more responsible for their actions. At the same time, however, cost-cutting measures make it more difficult for nurses to undertake the new responsibilities thrust on them and more difficult for them to practise the kinds of team approaches that the management has organized.

They're cutting the nurses. And they're calling us...all MRNs. You're the "Most Responsible Nurse," don't you know? And you're all MRNs. So when you get a crunch, i.e., you're all running six ways backwards and they want to send you two more patients, you're supposed to get together in this little huddle, you see–as if you have the time–and as a group you're making a decision as to who do you think could handle another patient, because you're all "most responsible nurses." I mean, it's wonderful on paper, but it's not functional because you're all too busy to get together in this little huddle and have a discussion. And besides, nobody wants another patient. They've all got too many now.

Individual nurses have been in the past, and continue to be, responsible for their own actions. This responsibility is part of their registration as nurses and the responsibility is enforced by their professional organization. The nurses are also responsible to doctors and patients. It has become increasingly difficult, however, for the nurses to work as their experience has taught, and their licence requires, to fulfill these responsibilities. The cutbacks and new ways of organizing work mean nurses

are stressed out 'cause they're operating at over 100 per cent continu-ously. So there's no respite...The patients are sped up because they have to get out for the next guy coming in. So they're failing...When does somebody start recognizing that this isn't what it was meant to be? Like who's handling this? But we still try to make it all better.

The nurses made it clear that they continue to feel responsible for their patients and try to provide the best care, in spite of the new conditions that make it increasingly difficult for them to act responsibly. Nurse after nurse said

You know every nurse at the bedside is trying and caring about the person...So even the fact there's not enough people there tomorrow, everybody still does as much as they can to help that individual patient. And the patients are always saying, "Oh, I can see you're so busy," and you're going, "Please tell me if something's wrong even though I'm busy. I can come. Otherwise we might miss it here." You know, they're trying to be so helpful too.

The problem is not simply that there is less money; it is also the way that new management systems have structured responsibility for nursing work. These problems are now camouflaged by the nurses' efforts to be responsible and exacerbated by managers who fail to understand this responsibility. When, for example, patient needs mean that nurses cannot get the job done in the time allowed, nurses "stay and we don't charge them 'cause they're telling us they won't pay any overtime." The unit manager says, "There is no money in the budget so I will not be paying overtime. So if you have to stay overtime you're going to have to take off when the wards are quiet." Such orders often come from "a physio or social worker manager" who has not taken the nurses' individual responsibility for patient care into account.

What she doesn't understand is if I was to perceive that the ward was quiet at 3:00 and I had worked half an hour overtime and I said to my buddies, "I'm going to go because I worked overtime yesterday," and one of my patients arrested and the outfall of that was that management saying, "Where is [the nurse's name]?" I could be fired for abandonment of my patient because I actually should have been there till 3:30.

Although the nurses continue to feel responsible as a group, they find it increasingly difficult when new systems hold them more individually responsible for patient care. The new management systems, they say, blame individual nurses when care is not provided, rather than examine the new reforms to see how the reforms limit the possibilities for providing care. These systems tend "to nail one individual nurse or group of nurses for saying that they didn't do a good job on Saturday night, three to eleven on October 26th," instead of recognizing that "the health care system is in crisis and we cannot continue to cut, cut, gut, gut and not lose what has been so important in Canada, and that's access to quality care for everybody."

Accountability through Advocacy

Nurses see patient advocacy as part of their responsibility as nurses, as part of their accountability. Some felt that they were still in a position to advocate for patients, although they often qualified this by pointing to their particular area. For example, one nurse said

> I feel that I am in a privileged position. I feel that I work in a place that usually still has enough nursing [staff], and that is because it's a high legal liability area and you have got to have nurses there. And I do advocate for patients...I can only advocate for day care people, but if they want to send them out and...I don't think they're ready to go, and they just need to sleep over night, whatever, I can have the autonomy that I can just put them down at the end of the hall and carry on.

Another reported that "we still have the power" to be patient advocates but cautioned that in terms of patient stays this was peculiar to "the acute-care parts of the hospital." She went on to say that "the 48-hour units do not have the power to stop the discharge process." Sometimes this advocacy involves an exchange of information or a discussion about what is best for the patient.

> When we talk to the most responsible nurse about discharge back to us it's a dialogue between the nurses. I mean, we say what we can cope with and they say what we need to cope with, and we come to a mutual decision that isn't overridden.

Physician support can be critical to this dialogue. In spite of the reforms, doctors retain considerable independence and the right to decide in matters that they and the nurses feel relate to the patient's interests. The nurses report that the doctors will "go with you" in advocating for longer patient stays. More than one nurse linked this independence to the doctors' relationship to the hospital. "I guess because they are not employees of the hospital, they don't have that real pressure to have to get them out." Doctors are nevertheless facing increasing pressure to rush patients through the system and to follow formulas that set out who gets to stay. But doctors are resisting, not only because they are independent of the hospital, but also because they are responsible to their own professional organizations. As one nurse explained,

> Some of the doctors here now are standing their ground on that because they're saying, "I'm not going to discharge this patient when they aren't ready to go home. And who's going to get sued if they go home and they get into trouble? Not the hospital because I'm the one who wrote the discharge order."

Conclusions on Accountable, Appropriate, Quality Care

The nurses interviewed for this project support *New Directions'* commitment to the appropriate use of health services, to the highest quality of care and to accountable services and providers. They also support many of the methods outlined in *New Directions*. The nurses are, however, concerned about what this commitment means in practice.

The goals seem to be undermined by the new emphasis on the assessment of quality and accountability through quantitative means, especially when this emphasis is combined with inappropriate measurement tools that fail to take either nursing skills or individual patients' needs sufficiently into account. The new standards and protocols recommended in the *New Directions* report risk quality care if they make it less possible for providers to base care not only on protocols but also on their own experience with the patient and their particular expertise. This is most likely to happen when practices developed in the for-profit production sector are applied to patient care, as is increasingly the case with the new managerial techniques. Yet health care is not like production work. As the nurses point out, "We're not talking about building widgets." These strategies taken from business can undermine the spirits of patients and providers, discouraging both and making quality care less likely. The nurses described their frustration with these practices in a variety of ways.

> I think that's why nursing morale is the way it is, is I think that that's what's happened. It's being looked at as a business and, you know, "utilization," how it all looks on paper. And the human touch is lost. In health care and in nursing it's nice to have care plans, but nobody fits into a care plan. And nobody fits into a time study because, like you

say, there's that human component. And I think that's what's happening with nursing is it's getting lost. And that's why nurses go into nursing is 'cause you want–you like being with people and you've got that empathy and you can't do that because they're telling you you've got five minutes to do this, you've got this, this.

It is not only a matter of morale but also of stress and fatigue caused by the heavy workloads based on new means of calculating care loads and patient care paths. "A lot of people are tired of work, just tired of being tired."

The nurses feel responsible–and are held responsible by their professional organizations–for their patients' health. This feeling of responsibility is evident not only in their words but also in their practices, in their struggles to keep up through working overtime and overly hard. Nurses are also increasingly held responsible by their employers through a variety of mechanisms, such as flattened hierarchies and patient satisfaction surveys. Yet they find it increasingly difficult to fulfill their responsibilities because new means of organizing and of monitoring the work too often get in the way.

The pressure on nurses has a visible impact on the quality of patient care. Although most nurses provided illustrations of declining quality from their experiences as providers, several based their assessment on their experience as patients. One nurse was particularly frustrated by the lack of control, which directly contradicts *New Directions'* promises to patients.

I kept likening myself to that lady in the next room with a stroke that they'd put in the wheel chair for the day out in the hall and took three hours to get the bed pan to her when she was calling for it and things like that. There's a total lack of control. And they only come around at 9:00 in the evening to give you ice water, or give you water to drink, or juice. If you're on forced fluids…that's it. And if you can't get out of bed to find the kitchenette to get yourself some juice or make it to the tap to fill your little plastic or paper glass up, you're out of luck for the next 24 hours until somebody comes into your room and does it for you. Not until the next time my meds were due. Or unless I could happen to hit the light button and then they'd call in and say, "What do you want?" And I'd tell them and they'd say, "Oh well, you're so and so's. I'll tell her." And then they're gone, and 20 minutes later…

Ironically, the technology that is supposed to enhance control can also serve to limit choice and human contact, as this nurse went on to explain. "I found when I was down for my surgery I was on the patient-controlled analgesic. So you see the nurse even less because you're not even calling to get anything for pain 'cause you're doing your own pain control." As a result, she "never saw them for hours and hours."

> Nobody checked my incision. I never got water. They'd bring you your tray and it's the food services that hands out the tray. So if your bedside table isn't close by, here's your food over here and you can't reach it. And it stays that way. And I hardly ate for the first couple days. My diet just kept progressing, you know. Instead of just leaving it on fluids more food kept coming. I wasn't eating it, but nobody had any idea.

She took some comfort in her nursing knowledge, in "the fact that I was physically able to get up and I understood why the tube was coming out of my neck and what I had to do to go to the bathroom, that sort of thing." Even though she knew how to assess her state and knew when she needed to call for help, she still found that "It's scary. I was glad that I regained consciousness and I was with it. The first thing I did was spit the tube out and start talking and I haven't stopped since because I've got something that I was threatened with losing." Like a number of her colleagues, she was convinced that quality was declining under the new reforms while providers became less accountable, primarily as a result of new ways of organizing the work, and of care that is less appropriate to patient needs.

While these stories provide only one kind of evidence about the ways reforms are influencing the quality of care, the nurses see very little reliable evidence being collected by management on the impact reforms have on quality. Such evaluation is necessary, as *New Directions* suggests, but the nurses stress that the evaluation must take the skills and knowledge of patients and providers into account. In moving towards what is called more accountable health care, "They're spending more time supporting the system than they are supporting people who are doing the caregiving."

Chapter 5

Health Promotion and the Prevention of Injury and Disease

Health promotion and disease prevention are strategies that date back more than a century. People involved in the public health movements of the nineteenth century struggled to prevent illness by ensuring safe water and food supplies, clean houses and better nutrition, limits on work time and improvements in working conditions. Florence Nightingale made good ventilation and clean hospitals central to her campaign for skilled nursing care. Combined with the sterilization of equipment, such strategies were a major factor in the transformation of hospitals from places the poor went to die to institutions that offered care and in many, if not most, cases, cures for people from all classes.

Although doctors and nurses were certainly involved in these efforts to improve health, the campaigns were not primarily about medicine. When immunization was introduced in the early 1900s, it marked the beginning of medical intervention techniques intended to prevent illness. For the most part, health promotion strategies were about factors beyond individual control. In the 1960s, however, the focus shifted more to the individual and to individual responsibility, with lifestyle and fitness as central concerns. More medically based techniques, such as pap smears, mammograms, x-rays and annual physical examinations, also grew in popularity, as did the idea of health promotion in general.

Throughout the 1980s, health promotion gained increasing prominence as a means of both encouraging wellness and reducing rising treatment costs. According to a recent book on these strategies, "Much–but not all–of the enthusiasm for health promotion has arisen from concern over spiraling health care expenditures."[244] Canada took a lead in this movement, claiming health promotion and disease prevention as a major feature of the approach to care. In British Columbia, *New Directions* promised that "**health promotion and the prevention of injury and illness** will receive greater attention"[245] (emphasis in original).

Prevention and Promotion Strategies That Work

The nurses interviewed for this study have seen some positive moves in the direction of health promotion and illness prevention. There are, for example, preventive health nursing offices that cover a range of programs. In larger cities, individual offices often specialize in particular health issues. Outside the major urban areas, "we aren't specialized, as an STD nurse or a school health nurse, or anything. We have to cover everything as it comes along, so we organize our own days." They do "immunizations that everybody here gets automatically for free and we even do hepatitis B now. They've done all of the kids up to grade 12." The mandate in these offices may be very broadly defined to encompass the full range of health determinants. In a sub-office, for instance, a nurse reports that "most of my time is spent in teaching and counselling community development and that's what I think of as health promotion, [disease] prevention."

British Columbia also uses nursing skills in determining whether environments are safe in various public spaces. While these jobs are not new, the number of nurses employed to do this work has increased in recent years and the definition of their work has expanded to match a new understanding of the factors that influence health. A nurse who does this kind of job explained the nature of her work in the following way:

> Traditionally my position as a licensing officer was a nursing position.
> It was sort of an offshoot of public health. That was their job, to go

around to the daycares and ensure health and safety issues, to advise on outbreaks, immunizations, things like that. And then it spread from there. It was too much for one to do. And that's where I came in. For a while there was only two of us doing it and it was very, very busy. Now there's seven of us doing it. And that's when they expanded it to include environmental health officers, because we don't deal strictly with nursing things. We might need to get the well water checked. We have to study floor plans for space if somebody wants to set up a new daycare. There's all these rules and regulations, provincial regulations to follow.

The licensing nurses now work in teams with people who have other kinds of training. "It's really complementary. There's only two nurses on staff and the others are ECE [Early Childhood Education] and social work…so what one doesn't know the other does…we even act as resources for each other." The result is a coordinated effort to establish an environment that promotes health.

Another example the nurses offered in relation to health promotion had to do with home care. Patients already in the system have a number to call where they can get help from a nurse who knows their particular case.

I would say that is one of the really good things. It sort of helps in the prevention and the promotion. Once they get a contact, like once we go out, they see me, you know, they have my card, they have the number. A lot of times it's prevent, you know they don't go to the hospital, you know things don't escalate because "Oh yeah, I'll phone," and then we'll put in that extra support in the short term to get them over that hump before it becomes a big crisis. But unfortunately you don't have contact with everybody. I mean, they have to be in the system and I have to go out and see them, but it certainly helps knowing that they have somebody. Especially the ones that have no family, that they're just alone here in the city.

Some of those who saw few immediate examples of prevention or promotion strategies were quite optimistic about the future in terms of an emphasis on health promotion.

When you look at the philosophy of our new health board, our new employers, you see much more written and you hear much more about [disease] prevention and [health] promotion because it's part of the continuum of health. And I think down the road we're probably going to see community health centres, not so much the fractionalization of the prevention program, home care, long-term care, all this. It'll be kind of a continuum of care and health promotion and prevention will be fused into everything.

But the nurses had more mixed assessments about how health promotion and injury and illness prevention were working in other areas.

Teaching Patients

Teaching is a core feature of prevention and promotion strategies. If people are to "take personal responsibility for good health habits" and "to make informed and effective decisions and choices" as the *New Directions* vision indicates, then teaching must be an integral feature of health care services.[246] Good health habits have to be learned, and nurses have a central role to play in that learning process. Indeed, teaching about health practices is explicitly included in their scope of practice. Similarly, if patients are to have more day surgery, if they are to be released from the hospital earlier and if they are to take more responsibility while they are in hospital, then they need to learn how to care for themselves and interpret their symptoms so that they know when it is appropriate to call for help.

These nurses have witnessed some useful teaching strategies. For example, they saw efforts being made to ensure that British Columbia's diverse population has information available in a variety of languages. One nurse is "on the diversity committee for the hospital" and reports that "there is a translator–interpreter services that you can call on short notice." Another said that

> for specific teaching we usually can find someone who can speak English. I can think of a young man who had a back fracture with no paralysis or anything and his brace was such that he wouldn't be able to get it on himself. He didn't need to wear it in bed, but it had to go on before he got out of bed in the morning and we finally found a brother-in-law who could speak English, and this guy lived with his mother, who was going to be putting the brace on. So they all came in together and I taught them, you know. But those are specific teaching things, but other just sort of generalized promotion of health care and wellness, for those it's very difficult.

Indeed, more information in print and video form is available to all patients. In a large hospital, there is a family/patient resource centre. And it's there for people that have questions. Patients or the family have questions and you contact this resource centre and there's a librarian and there's an RN in there. And I mean, I would have found it very helpful for my father because, being that Mom was never admitted to a hospital, he never had any resources on pancreatic cancer except for me.

However, the nurse who had this positive experience was also concerned that this centre would become a substitute for, rather than a complement to, nurses providing information to individual patients in their care. She went on to say, "But I guess this is now going to fill in the gap of patients that are discharged early so therefore they can phone the patient/family resource centre and get information that the nurse probably was teaching them on the unit." Another nurse added that the centre is

only open during the daytime…three or four hours a day. So you see, on the surface it looks really nice that that's happened and I'm thinking, well that's great. And now suddenly I'm thinking, hang on. That's for that poor patient that got discharged early…or [the patient who] is coming in four weeks from their pre-admit appointment to be admitted.

In the past "the nurse used to be able to do that." In the patient resource centre,

They have a registered nurse on the ground floor of this big, big house, and that's where people get sent. They come in for pre-admission now, as you know, because they don't come in and go overnight. And if they have any questions that can't be answered in pre-admission because they don't have time, then they get sent to this patient resource. There's one person and ten million pamphlets, and that's what they get. They get another pat on the back and another smiling face and here's another pamphlet and sit and read it and I'll answer any questions you have. It's like…Shoppers Drug Mart. It's stop and shop.

While the videos and print information can be useful, increasingly often they are the only instructions the patients get because the nurses have no time to help them understand the material and to help ensure that patients can interpret this material in terms of their own situation.

You're supposed to actually be with the patient while they and the family watch the video and then you're supposed to talk about it. Well, we don't have time to sit and watch the video while the rest of our 19 patients need things on the ward, so off they go with the video. If they have any questions, they can ask them. Most often they don't.

The nurses have witnessed an erosion of teaching, a gradual progression from the videos being part of an education package that involved individual teaching to the videos and books providing the only education.

We've done it for years in open heart. They watch a pre-op video before your heart surgery and then afterwards, after you have surgery, if you had a valve you have to watch *Living with Your Valve*, anticoagulant therapy. We have a nutrition one, *Heart to Heart*, if they want to watch it. They have to watch the other before we let them go home. And they have a book that's given to them in the beginning. If they have questions they can ask us. It used to be we would sit down and go through the book with them and talk about it and really be there for any questions, like "When can I have sex?" you know. We just don't have time.

The nurses' instructions cannot easily be replaced by these other learning aids. For one thing, the patients might not be able to comprehend the instructions. This is particularly a problem for those who do not read or understand either official language or who have no close relatives to provide interpretation and other assistance. The following is just one example of the problem.

I had a poor old fellow who was so sweet and he was going home to live on his own and finally he had to say to me ('cause I joke along with them. You know: "You have to read your book. I'm going to give you a test before I let you out the door.") And finally he looks at me, two big tears in his eyes, and he says, "I can't read." So I sat down with him. Everybody else went on hold, and it was a full bed ward and the other patients heard him say it, so they were really good about letting me spend some time with him. Other languages, we try and get interpreters to come in. But normally we have to use the family. There's got to be someone in the family that speaks English so we just tell them that person has to come up and watch the video.

Language is not the only barrier to comprehension of materials introduced as a substitute for learning with a trained care provider. People who are under a great deal of stress are often not in a position to take in what the instructions say. When the diagnosis is given, "They only hear 20 per cent of what they were told in the office that day because they were so stressed out." For those patients facing surgery, instructions are now given at pre-admission sessions that often happen four weeks before the patients actually enter the hospital. As a result, the instructions could be forgotten or the time lapse can make the information irrelevant. Citing this method of teaching surgical patients, a nurse said

> We have a lot of problems with that too, because the patients will come to the pre-admit clinic and it might be four weeks before they get in for surgery and lots of things can happen in four weeks. But they come to pre-admit clinic, they get a tick-off sheet, the nurse gets them ready for the OR, an IV shoved in them, they may be asked, "Has anything happened in your life in the last four weeks?" Most of them say "No." They go for their surgery. They have an MI [myocardial infarction] on the table or…full-blown DTs [delirium tremens, or alcohol-induced hallucinating]. We've had that. Because there's lots of things have happened in four weeks.

Before the most recent reforms, patients booked for most surgery were admitted to the hospital the day before. As this same nurse went on to explain, "If they'd come in the night before, we'd probably, between the nurses and the residents admitting them, would have picked up on a few things." A second nurse added

> What happened when people had to come in the night before, you saw that they fasted, you could watch them. You saw that they didn't drink alcohol or if they were going to go into the DTs or into drug withdrawal you could catch these things. You can't do any of that now when they're in day surgery. I mean, one guy came in and I could smell the whiskey from outside before he came in. And he came in for a liver biopsy. That makes a lot a sense, I have to tell you. I mean, I knew he was the liver biopsy. I said to someone, "That liver biopsy patient's late" and I said, "I smell whiskey," and in he came through the door. She goes, "Oh good, a cancellation." I mean literally, don't you think– years ago we used to shave them the night before, we used to watch them…We used to do all kinds of things that you cannot do now. And they recovered better…You could talk to them about the procedure. And they didn't come back.

The strategy of transferring almost everyone to day surgery or out-patient clinics is often inefficient as well as contrary to the health promotion goal.

They don't seem to see that coming back increases the cost because they're processed through twice. You do all the intake and all the whatever, and they're in and then you do all the out, and then next thing you know you're doing it all...again. It's ridiculous.

These nurses were not arguing that we should return to admitting all patients the night before. Rather, they blame the problems on the "rush, rush, rush," on "not enough explanation given to the family" and on strategies that apply the same rules to everyone, regardless of their capacity to understand and follow the instructions. Some people might need to be admitted the night before, while others may be able to understand and follow the instructions provided under the new systems. Learning takes time and so does the process of determining who needs more instruction or a different approach.

And you know, when you ask the patient something like, "has anything happened in the last four weeks?" (a) they're anxious because they've come in the day of their surgery, and (b) they don't know exactly what you mean. They don't know. This is one thing that's come up in this doctor's office when I've done medical histories. I've asked the patient, "Have you had any problem?" after they've had a surgical procedure. And they say, "Well, no, no," and then they say, "What do you mean problem?" And then you have time to explore it. And you can come up with some really weird things the patient thought was not a complication at all. And this is the thing. You're admitting how many people on same-day admit? You haven't got time to sit down and say, "Listen, are you sure?" You're missing that information. You don't have time to ask them.

Moreover, learning has to happen when the patient is willing and able to learn, and indeed able to learn a great deal of vital information.

There is an issue here of client readiness. And the one thing about teaching is that people have to be ready to learn. And when you're in the middle of an acute intervention or in a nearly hypoxic [state] or really high [on a] drug, like morphine analgesic level post-operatively, you're not in a place where you're going to learn anything. And you know, they say that a great deal, depending on which researcher you're reading, of the causation of cardiovascular disease has to do with modifiable things. And so, you know, they're sending people out of the hospital before you have a chance to work with them on some of that stuff. And so they're going home with huge wounds that are barely healed. They just pulled the staples out. They may be gaping and they have wound care that they have to deal with. They have to deal with increasing activity. They may have a new pacemaker that they never had before, plus they've got all the stuff they had before. Smoking, exercise, diet, you know, understanding how family history relates to this hypertension, diabetes. They've got all that stuff happening to them still, but they go home.

Both the limited time available on day surgery, and new management strategies that specify when learning is to happen, make it increasingly difficult for nurses to teach when the patient is ready to learn.

It is not only day surgery that limits the learning time. It is also the pressure of heavy patient loads. In the past, the variety in patient acuity levels "gave you the leeway to do the teaching too because you have a couple of sick patients but you have other patients that were self-sufficient." Now, with patients leaving quicker and sicker, there is virtually no opportunity to determine whether they have in fact learned what is necessary for the rest of their care.

They've got all kinds of pamphlets, too, that ideally you would want to give to them, review with them, have them read them, ask questions, go back at another time and check to see what they've retained of that, or what they can put into practice in their lives, discuss it with their families. But often they're not there long enough to do that progressive assessment of how much they're keeping in and what they're learning. And sometimes they're too sick just to take it in. I mean, I've put videos on for cardiac patients pre-discharge and they fall asleep during them. So you know that they didn't get anything out of that one. You know, this might be how to detect the signs of angina when they go home again...some really important stuff.

There is little space left for teaching when patients are ready to learn, and the timing does not often fit the format envisaged by those preparing learning materials, as one nurse eloquently explained.

I work in the spinal cord intensive-care unit, very specialized area, and our patient population is very, very sick and they've had a very traumatic event happen to them. And there is a tremendous learning curve that they go through. We have huge learning packages...All these media and all this great teaching material to present to our patient population, but I mean, rare is the day that I get more than five minutes a day to spend with a patient, and I have a low patient ratio. Sometimes

I'm only looking after one patient and sometimes two patients. But even with that patient ratio, rare is the opportunity I get to teach and that's usually when I'm doing the tub, you know, so I can't sort of go and get my foot charts and my material. As I'm giving my bath I'm doing my teaching. You find ways to work it in, but certainly they are nowhere near where I think they should be by the time [they leave].

When patient stays are shortened, patients are often not ready to learn or to take over care tasks from the nurses.

You can see that in the maternity unit. I mean, with breast feeding the babies. Often the mother's milk doesn't come in until 48 hours or whatever and now mom's home. So what happens now [is that] this nurse is never going to be able to teach a mother or know what it's like when the milk starts to come in and how the baby knows and the mother knows and everything, because she's not going to be seeing it. She's not going to see it.

A few nurses did say that "In our unit, we do a lot of teaching; we've got time and our patients are in for a couple of months." But most nurses have less time to teach, just as teaching is becoming more important. "They want us to do a ton of teaching but they don't give you the time to do it. I find that frustrating…A lot of the wards send patients home and they haven't taught them a thing 'cause they haven't had time."

More and more of the teaching work that does get done is performed by those with less and less training for the job. Fewer of those with special teaching skills are hired. Take the example of diabetes education:

What really bothers me is right now we have diabetic educators who are absolutely wonderful and it's a requirement that they have passed the Canadian Diabetic Association exams and most of them have their degree. And if we have a new diabetic in-patient or a diabetic that's going onto insulin or something, the diabetic educator will come up and spend the time, sometimes two and three hours, with these poor old people that are 75 years old and now on insulin. And they're saying now, "Oh, there's no money for a diabetic educator," so they've put out a document which I haven't seen yet, and it's, I forget what they call it, survival, the survival kit for the bedside nurse of the diabetic, so that we can now teach the patients and send them home. This just doesn't make sense to me that on the one hand you require someone with a degree who's got to pass some Canadian Diabetic Association exam and all of a sudden it's fine for me who hasn't taught diabetes for eons, especially not to a 75-year-old who's just had open-heart surgery.

Registered nurses increasingly expect that teaching will be part of their job, but they might not have the preparation for these quite special cases. At the same time as they are being expected to take over from these specialists, they find more of their traditional teaching work passed on to those with less formal education. Before the current wave of reforms, community-care nurses were able to devote a significant proportion of their time to teaching in combination with their other nursing activities.

At that time we mainly looked after elderly clients who had ulcers or needed a bath or needed diabetic teaching, and we don't see hardly any of those patients anymore because the baths are all done by homemakers and the ulcers we seem to deal with much better because of new products, and we teach all the patients to do their own insulin. But now we're seeing patients who are needing IVs in the community for antibiotic treatment or whatever. We give chemotherapy in the community. We've got patients on respirators in the community.

The nurses find it increasingly difficult to have their teaching recognized and counted as part of essential services under the new reforms. So part of their teaching involves teaching the new managers about what counts as prevention. As one nurse involved directly in community prevention programs put it,

I think part of the challenge for us in prevention is getting the message across to the regional health board that we're performing a function, a nursing function, when it's not measurable. It's not measurable in immediate terms, anyway. And some of it is never measurable. [It's] very hard to define our job.

The new reforms, which place more responsibility for care on patients and their families, which shorten the lengths of time that nurses have to assess the effectiveness of the care provided to each patient, and which increase nursing workloads, mean that teaching and learning have become even more essential. Nurses find, however, that they have even less time for the kind of teaching and that their patients have even fewer opportunities for the kind of learning that effectively promote health and prevent further disease and injury. The print and video materials now available all too often serve as an inadequate substitute for direct nurse–patient teaching and learning, rather than serving as a supplement to this process.

Clean and Safe Environments

A clean environment has long been recognized as central to good health. This is particularly the case in health care institutions, where people often have more vicious germs to spread and are more vulnerable to infection. In the new managerial strategies, however, cleanliness is seldom defined as part of health care or even part of prevention. Instead, cleaning services are often redefined as hotel services and severely cut back or altered to bring them more in line with methods used in other sectors.

The nurses have witnessed significant changes in cleaning as a result of reforms. Emergency rooms provide a particularly telling example of the move away from a focus on a sterile environment.

> Well, I'll tell you when I worked in emergency about 20 years ago, every stretcher was washed after every patient...When I worked at emergency about eight years ago, the bed stretchers were washed once per shift. You know, the linen was changed but there was no actual washing unless somebody happened to notice the blood on the rail. And now in the emergency at the hospital where I am now, they're washed once a day. And that's it. We still happen to be closed at night time so that's when we get them washed down. And unless somebody happens to see, and I can tell you in the emergency department, being so busy, it's not likely that a nurse is going to notice that there's blood on the rail until later in the day or till the thing is actually [complained about]. And that's because there aren't the number of people that used to be there. It doesn't seem to be a priority and I don't know how you expect people to get well when they're in a contaminated environment.

Cleaning is frequently identified by management as an area in which costs can be reduced. The cleaning tasks may be recognized as necessary, but they do not necessarily get accomplished, despite the best efforts of the cleaning people who remain. As more than one nurse explained, "They still make lists out for the cleaning staff." However, "when they are short then you eliminate these jobs and only do these jobs. The cleaners still try and do all the things on their list but they have two wards to cover instead of one and then they're getting injured." As this statement demonstrates, the problem is not restricted to emergency rooms. Another example came from a cardiovascular unit.

> Our housekeeping staff works as hard as they can, but our director [says that]...you have to have Mr. So-and-So, 85, five days post-op, open heart, out of that bed and the bed made by 9:00 a.m. And the

doctor's just arrived at 8:30 to give him the 16 medications on this prescription that you have to go over. So the beds are barely–I mean they don't have time to cool down before the guy's coming out from ICU to fill it.

The rapid patient turnover is combined with reductions in housekeeping staff. A number of nurses reported that "We no longer have housecleaning, except for emergency. One guy on a pager evenings and nights, weekends, statutory holidays, and reduced-activity days. The units only have emergency housekeeping." Nurse after nurse said

that's why our infections rate is going up too, one of the reasons. Now they've taken away all the housekeeping staff so the nurses end up washing the beds sloppily to get somebody in to it or they don't wash it at all 'cause it's not their job and they're just saying, "To hell with it."

The reduction in cleaning not only denies the commitment to prevention; it is also inefficient. Very expensive personnel, and their anxious patients, may have to wait for cleaning to be done because there are fewer housekeeping staff around to do even the minimum cleaning work.

It takes a lot longer to get cleaners, too. For instance, in a unit where there's high turnover, and where there's turnover and you need to get a patient out 'cause another patient is coming in, it takes a lot longer to get someone up there to clean the bed. Sometimes the patients arrive without a bed to go into because you won't put them in a bed that hasn't been cleaned because you know what was in it before the patient came.

Lots of the germ-containing dirt that is not cleaned up is invisible. But the cleaning has deteriorated to such an extent that the nurses say that now even the patients are noticing it. One nurse reported that "They had a great big poster in the hallway that gave the results of the patient survey and [it] had this graph that showed you they were 90 per cent happy with the staff and only 75 per cent as far as the cleanliness."

As more patients are sent home with open wounds or in other states that put them in the high-risk category for infection, the nurses also worry about conditions in the home. It is difficult for many people to keep their homes in an appropriate sterile condition, even if they know how. It is also difficult in the home to prevent infections from spreading to other family members, and it is difficult for individual households to find means of waste disposal that conform to the kinds of standards set out for hospitals. Morever, people with open wounds are not the only ones who need help ensuring that they have clean surroundings. This kind of service is also required by people who are frail and elderly, or are disabled. Yet the public system is providing fewer cleaning services for all of these people.

> About three years ago part of our program was that we would supply cleaning services. If someone, say, had arthritis or mobility problems or whatever and couldn't manage to keep their house tidy we would send someone in for maybe a couple hours a week to scrub the bathroom floors and [do] sort of the heavier cleaning. And because of cutbacks with money they decided that we would no longer do cleaning. So as case managers we had to get on the phone and call all these clients and explain to them why they could no longer get this cleaning service and that was quite a to-do. But that was sort of the start of it.

These nurses define cleanliness as a critical component in prevention strategies. Indeed, they see infections that are resistant to antibiotics appearing with alarming speed. They see more and more of the people admitted to institutions experiencing multiple health problems, problems that make them very vulnerable to infection. And they see a rapid increase in the number of people who are sent home long before they have built up their immune systems. While all these trends mean that cleanliness is even more important, they see fewer resources allocated to cleaning services and less attention paid to the quality of the services that remain. Most nurses agreed that "the policies for isolation are quite good" and that these policies are particularly important in areas where street drugs or tuberculosis and other communicable diseases are common. But they see less attention paid to the less clearly medical methods for preventing the spread of disease.

Respecting the Care Provider

New Directions promised "prevention strategies to address abuse of providers in the workplace and to ensure a safe working environment."[247] Initiatives such as the Labour Adjustment Plan that promise to relocate providers have helped alleviate a portion of the insecurity caused by restructuring, and thus helped relieve some stress on the workers. But many of the nurses we interviewed feel abused by other new reform strategies.

The work speed-up caused by early discharge and day surgery leaves nurses exhausted. Nurses throughout the system had this complaint. One nurse, who does not work in intensive or emergency care, the areas most associated with high work pressure, describes her situation:

> Well, the patient acuity has just escalated. My area is basically reconstructive orthopedics, and for example, our knee patients would stay until they had an 85-degree bend. And now that doesn't matter. They go home post-op Day Five. An 85-degree bend might not have occurred for three weeks if they stayed. But now–and the hip patients stayed for 12 days and now they stay for six. So we've always got patients from zero to six days post op. So it's much busier.

Reports of burnout and illness resulting from overwork were common in these interviews.

> There is a high turnover, particularly in the care aides. They really get injured and sick...I'm seeing lots of sickness. I mean, the management asked us to maintain standards...It's basically impossible to do that. Even as a nurse you're stressed and the next thing you're going to go on stress leave, or your blood pressure gets sky-high or stuff like that, and I notice the more frustration people have, the heavier the workload, the more often they go on sick [leave] for one reason or another. Some people basically call in sick because they have a problem with administration.

Reports of injuries resulting from the new organization of work were also common and were related to the entire range of reforms.

> They have people reporting in sick. So often they have lots of injuries because when they are lifting by themselves sometimes you can't help it. I remember an incident when I was working at the place which is a problem, and I had two care aides at that time. We had to send one care aide to help to wash dishes in the kitchen because they were–according to our administrator, she had to reduce staff in the dietary department...the care aides had to go to the kitchen to wash dishes. One of the care aides was on coffee break, another was in the dietary department washing dishes. I was alone on the floor when a resident fell down. I had nobody to help me. I basically had to stand there, send one of the relatives to look for the care aide and it took at least 15 to 20 minutes for them to arrive and we were only two and she's a huge lady. Even [if] it's not so drastic, even if you have two care aides on the floor in the evening, if somebody was about to fall down, we have three

wings, two floors, even if I shout they will not hear. So sometimes I injured my back like that because I have to support that patient who was about to fall down. And I have the injury, and I was on Workmen's Compensation. It was about one month, one and a half months.

Within institutions, the nurses report that the growing number of injuries could be prevented if there were enough staff and enough time to use appropriate equipment and techniques. With more nurses working in the community, however, it is more difficult to ensure support, and these nurses usually work alone. They are thus at a greater risk of injury. "There is a problem vis-à-vis lifting, that you might not have anybody to help you." Even if another person is present, that person is unlikely to have the necessary skills to provide safe assistance.

The risk not only comes from patients and workloads. It also comes from workplaces designed for other times and ways of organizing care. The new computer systems, for example, have often simply been placed within old workstations or placed in new ones without regard for ergonomics and without consulting the nurses who use them.

How do you save money when they go and put all these new computers in at the nursing stations when these nursing stations were designed 30, 40 years ago for nurses to sit? They don't ever design a desk for a nurse to sit at, so now they put a computer in a place that is ergonomically a disaster. And now what's happening is that they're making them sit in these horrible chairs, to sit and do the charting and the computer work and you're now increasing injuries. But do they have the nurses in there to consult when they build the new buildings? No.

The overcrowding that results from the high turnover and cutbacks also adds to the risk.

There is more stress... The unit, the nursing station where we are, was built and made for a family practice unit who had four nurses, a unit clerk, and a head nurse. Now we have six MSIs [medical-surgical interns, year one], about eight residents, the two attending physicians plus the people who come for consults. Plus six nurses.

Many nurses want to leave nursing as a result of the speed-up and other reforms. More than one nurse said, "I could count the months till I can quit 'cause I don't like what's happened. I don't. I'm getting too old for the pace that nursing has become. I just can't keep up with it physically."

The exhaustion is exacerbated when nurses have less control over when their patients leave and over how much care those patients receive. They also have less control over their own work hours.

Because of the acuity of the patients, they come in and they survive their initial accident or their health crisis and they're sicker on the unit, where ten, twelve years ago they wouldn't even be coming into acute care. They'd be going straight to an ICU or a critical-care area. The nurses work flat out. They send the patients home knowing they're not well enough to go home. They're not having the support from the managers and administrators to get extra help. We don't have a lot of problems on our unit getting in sick relief and vacation relief. A lot of nurses want to come to our unit because it's just, "Oh, I can get away from all of that." But I know other units the nurses are working, the critical-care areas are working overtime and days off and they're just exhausted. And they're not happy with what they're doing.

Research on workers' health has demonstrated that control over work is an important determinant of health.[248] It is central to health promotion and to the maintenance of health among workers. Yet reforms mean less control for nurses. Nurses face greater restrictions and more managers who do not understand nursing work, but who do embrace new managerial strategies taken from the for-profit sector. The consequence, the nurses say, is both poorer health and higher costs.

Another issue…I think is very important [is] the environment which you work in, if you are trusted. If people believe in you, if you are encouraged to produce much better work. If you have a person who is policing you all the time and who is there to blast you for basically very, very small problems, then you feel that you are walking on thin ice all the time. And that's exactly what I was discussing with two staff yesterday. Both of them, they say that if they can have another job they will be out of this facility. Basically it is not possible to have a job. And I think such an environment affects the care. If you are not happy, if you are afraid, if you are intimidated, you don't put all your mind to work and I don't understand why management would be stupid. It's not productive for them. They have high turnover of staff, they have sickness, the rate of the sickness goes sky-high, they have a place where the staff basically don't produce best in their quality of work. I really cannot understand what they gain with such an attitude.

The loss of control is not universal, however. Some nurses said that the management, and conditions, did allow them both more control and more respect. For example, one long-term care nurse described her situation as better than in other institutions where she had worked because

> First of all the staffing level is slightly better. They have 45 patients for a nurse. We have also management who is not sitting on your back. They left you alone and they trust you more as a professional. They trust you to make decisions. And there, the workload in general is much less than in the other facility, but the main thing is the atmosphere which they create.

Her situation demonstrated that it was possible to create the safe working environment *New Directions* promised, but not if staff are overworked and if trust is not the basis for working relationships. One nurse eloquently summarized the views of many when she said, "The care for the caregiver, I think, has never been there and it's getting worse."

Promoting Patient Health

When nurses have greater control over their work, it is not only the nurses who are healthier; their patients are as well. The nurses see the threat to their patients as the work speeds up, their exhaustion increases and their control declines. This threat takes a number of forms.

When the turnover among nurses is high, and when they work at high speed, it can mean that the nurses do not know their patients. "It's very dangerous. In fact, for that matter, even people who work fairly often there, they don't remember exactly the names or the faces sufficiently; you can make a mistake." The patients might not even be sure of their own identities, either, and there may be no time to make other checks. Formulas for care that assume a standard patient can make matters worse.

> If you have to give medication to 75 people and you are new or you are fairly new in that facility, there is no way you can, in one hour and a half, give medication to those people without danger of making a mistake. And plus, it's our job to check the right name, the right person, and the right drug. Our people, quite a number of them are confused. "Are you Mrs. Smith?" She'll tell you, "Oh yes, I am." But she's not. That is not reliable information, to ask the patient about her name. If you are working in a facility where people are in a normal frame of mind, maybe. But not in extended care.

The problem seems obvious to the nurses we interviewed. "If she has 75 people and she has to do several dressings, there is no way she can do it properly."

In addition to the obvious danger of mistakes, there is the less obvious danger related to the failure to provide adequate care or to prevent illness. This is particularly clear in long-term care institutions.

> Well, I mean an example will be if there is only one nurse, if somebody has infection it's overlooked. Whatever it is, if it's urinary infection or anything. We have to call the doctor much more often. If that person had–first of all if that person was washed well, properly, peri care and stuff like that are very important matters, probably the care aides or even the nurses sometimes…could have introduced that infection. Secondly, in other stages of infection you can encourage them with fluids. You can prevent that infection from escalating. You can look after their diet better maybe, that you know they're well nourished so that they can fight the infection. And most of the time when infection is noticed is when the resident becomes totally agitated and starts throwing things and maybe even injuring somebody, that's the time you say, "Oh gee, what's happening with him?" And that's the time only maybe you realize there is a physical problem which is correlated to that.

The lack of care might save money in the short run, but it often leads to increased costs in the long run.

> It means antibiotics, the doctor is there a couple of times at least. And of course more work for the staff working around that person when he is more sick. And even more often they have to go to the hospital. So I mean, it's so obvious [that it will] cost. When you have a nurse who will prevent it, who will recognize other symptoms, and when you don't have a nurse or when you ship that person from the hospital, maybe the facility where we are working will not pay but the government will pay for the doctor, for the pharmacy bill, for the hospital, much more than they would pay for the nurse.

Basic, time-proven prevention strategies may be sacrificed in the rush to provide the prescribed medical treatment. Just one of the many examples came from eye care: "I mean…we have…so little time to give eye drops…Basically, we have to wash our hands each time we give the eye drops. Sometimes you have to choose. Either you wash your hands or you don't give the eye drops."

Conclusions on Health Promotion and the Prevention of Injury and Disease

New Directions identified health promotion and the prevention of injury and illness as one of its goals. The nurses do see a continuing commitment to medical interventions such as immunization, and some enhancement of efforts in areas such as the inspection of daycare centres. However, they also see cutbacks in all sorts of areas that are having a negative impact on health.

> The problems we're seeing in families now [are] just so much more and worse than ten years ago. And we see families who, you know, they don't have any money. They don't have any work. They're hungry. They're having a hard time relationship-wise. They're having a hard time dealing with the kids. They're having a hard time making decisions, and it's just really different. And they have a hard time dealing with the nurses in the hospital. So there's more demands and occasionally outbursts, and just—we've seen a real escalation in the amount of violence and child abuse and things like that.

The concentration of many services in megahospitals in major cities limits patients' access to the support that is critical to health promotion. As one nurse explained,

> The family has a big part in how you recuperate. I mean, depending if you have a relationship with your family. But you know people that do, they want their family near them... We hear that from people that come from [outside the city] that have to come down for surgery or to have a baby if it's a difficulty that wasn't anticipated. I mean, it's pretty lonely being there all by yourself.

The reductions in services are undermining prevention and promotion strategies within health care.

> We're called case managers but now we're becoming more crisis management because, you know, our caseloads are so high and the people are much more ill and it takes us longer to deal with people. But you know there certainly is a lot on my caseload that we are doing, you know. Education and health promotion. But not to the level that we'd like to see, and a lot of that has to do with some of the wait list. Like for instance if I go out and see an elderly person and you know, they're doing not too badly, but I think they're kind of isolated socially, maybe

they don't have family, whatever, they're not getting out and I think it would be great for them to go into the adult day care centres and they agree. They know they'd like to get out and everything else. Well, I put them on my list and again it's five, six months before they get in. Well in that five to six months when you're 80 years old, anything could happen. And so here we're trying to prevent something, we're trying to provide a quality of life for this elderly person and then because the resources aren't there, there's not enough of them, something happens. They fall, they break their hip, or they catch pneumonia, you know, something. And so then we're in there as a crisis thing again.

Within health care institutions, the nurses do not see much of an increased emphasis on prevention strategies for patients or providers. There are more teaching materials in print and video form, and more centres provide information to patients. But what patients mainly see are dirtier institutions and homes in spite of the evidence demonstrating that cleanliness is critical to care, and most importantly, they see rushed nurses who have less time to do the basic preventive work, often at the expense of themselves and their patients.

Conclusion

The context for health care reform has changed dramatically since public care was introduced in Canada. This context both shapes, and is shaped by, practices here at home. Globally, policies promoting the market prevail. Locally, there is still strong support among both citizens and many politicians for a public system based on notions of shared responsibility and collective rights, rather than on individual consumer choice and purchasing power.

However, even those reforms undertaken in the name of preserving public care are based on models taken from the for-profit sector and on market practices. This adoption of market and managerial strategies has been based primarily on faith rather than on evidence. At the same time, evidence and accountability are said to be at the centre of new approaches to care.

Our research with British Columbia nurses was designed to analyse their assessments of the claims made for health care reforms. In the interviews, the nurses made it clear that they support the overall goals set out in *New Directions*. Indeed, they have promoted efforts to make care more integrated and to enhance continuity, especially through an emphasis on primary care offered in community clinics. They recognize that quality should be a primary concern and that greater accountability through public participation can help make care delivery more responsive to patient and provider needs. Nurses have long been committed to the health promotion and the injury and disease prevention that they see as part of their job, and they would welcome an increased emphasis on these elements. What they do not see is these goals being fulfilled by the current reforms.

In the course of the group interviews, the nurses did identify positive aspects of the reforms. They recognize, for example, that it makes sense to do complicated eye surgery in a central location where the most skilled people with the best equipment can do the work. And it makes sense to use day surgery for people who can be easily taught the necessary pre- and post-operative care, and who have safe environments for recovery at home. However, they also identified some fundamental flaws.

One important flaw is that reformers fail to recognize the skilled nature of nursing work and to make nurses' experiences central to reform. Nurses do the bulk of health care work and they spend the most time with patients. Yet the new managerial strategies fail to recognize important aspects of their work or to consult them in effective ways about how to change the work. As one long-term care nurse explained, the nurses are in a position to see what the doctors and managers do not see.

> I think that if you don't [know nursing work], you have absolutely no idea where you're going. I think one of the big things that we forget and that is not recognized with nurses–and it always annoys me that it isn't– is that nurses, every nurse, like you said, when you see a patient you're doing all kinds of things that tell you where the patient is at, and nurses not only do things that the doctor has ordered, but they see things that the doctor never sees. You know, the old subdural hematoma, four times to hospital, four times sent back saying, "He's just fine." And he still has the chunk out of his head six months later because they couldn't fit it back in. And each one of the things I think you do because the doctor isn't there all the time. And that seems to get lost. I often wonder where these politicians are in hospitals. You know. Like where is the nurse who was saying, "Excuse me, there's been cuts and so you realize that from now till the next four hours down the road don't be asking for anything because I have other people to deal with."

Important aspects of skilled care are lost in the new managerial strategies, and so are important ways to not only improve the quality of care but also to reduce costs in the long run. Too often accountability is defined in terms of counting. Such counting usually ignores critical care components that can prevent both poor health outcomes and expenditure increases. The systems are designed more to reduce costs and control providers than they are to improve continuity and promote quality care. "They don't follow that patient. That's the thing. It stops when he goes out the door. And he goes back" to incur more costs, and at the expense of his health.

A second, equally important flaw is the emphasis on a single managerial strategy for reform. Formulas for integration, for care assessment, for nursing staff workloads, for home care, for day surgery, for teaching, for all aspects of health care, are based on the assumption of a standard patient, standard provider and a single right way to provide care. But, as these nurses point out, very little is standard in practice. The formulas fail to take the individual differences among patients into account and fail to allow providers the discretion they must have if they are to respond to these individual needs.[249]

A third, and related flaw, is the rush to reform. The speed of reform leaves little opportunity to adequately assess the consequences. In the process, it creates insecurity that causes high levels of stress among both patients and providers.

And finally, the reforms often fail to apply lessons about prevention either to the provision of care or to the care providers. Safe environments are critical to health; so are secure relations at work that offer some control to the providers. Progress has been made in terms of employment security for some workers, but too many of the reforms result in increased stress, illness and injury for providers, while putting more patients at risk.

In short, nurses support reform, but they see the practices as a long way from the promises. The result, they fear, could be an undermining of public health care and of their own health.

Appendix A
A Note on Methods

The Interviews

Almost all of the information in this report comes from ten group interviews conducted during October 1997 with a total of 39 Registered Nurses working in British Columbia. In a typical interview, three to five nurses would spend a little over two hours discussing with both Pat Armstrong and Hugh Armstrong how health reform and health care are being managed. To help ensure that nothing was lost from what turned out to be lively, even passionate conversations, two tape recorders were used in each session.

The nurses came to the interviews from a wide range of health care settings. These included intensive care units in hospitals and public health units in communities, general medical/surgical wards and long-term care nursing, home health and emergency rooms, out-patient surgery and nurse practitioners. The interviews were conducted entirely away from their places of work. Almost all of those interviewed had at least 10 years of nursing experience. Most began their careers as RNs, but some had started as Practical Nurses and had become RNs only subsequently. Several had two or more university degrees, and a few had been educated and/or had nursed outside Canada. In addition, a few had worked in or were now working in supervisory positions. Many worked full-time, others part-time.

They were brought together for the group interviews by the British Columbia Nurses' Union (BCNU). They were not however recruited on the basis of union activism, but rather as volunteers who could provide the researchers with a rich variety of experiences and perspectives on health care. Most were recruited by responding to announcements placed on BCNU notice boards at their workplaces. In order for the researchers to gain access specifically to union perspectives on health care and its reform, one of the sessions involved several hands-on nurses who also held elected positions at the regional level in the BCNU. Interestingly, at this session the discussion on the position of nurses in the face of changes to health care was particularly lively.

To start each session, the researchers explained the project's purposes and processes, and then invited questions and discussion about the interviews to follow. Participants were told that they could refuse to answer any question and could withdraw from the interview at any time. (None did so.) The measures for ensuring that their identity or that of their employer remained confidential were set out. All participants received and signed consent forms that also specified how they could reach the research team after the interview, and what would happen to the research findings. A copy of the consent form is included as Appendix B.

The Research Questions

The research was designed to assess **how health care and its reform actually work from the vantage point of those most involved in providing this care: Registered**

Nurses. Certainly the research team's questions and analyses have been informed by what has been written on this subject by legislators and other public policy makers, by management theorists and consultants, by social scientists, by health care providers and administrators, by unions, and by journalists, as well as by the team's own previous research on health care. But at the core of this study is the information provided during the ten group interviews. In these sessions, 39 experienced nurses generously shared their stories, their perceptions and their insights on how the ideas, structures and policy directives that frame health care in the province get translated into actual caring work. Or don't get translated, for on many an occasion the official policy proves to be unworkable or contradictory or even harmful.

The researchers asked the nurses to address issues of the appropriateness, accountability and quality of the care they and others provide, the extent to which it is integrated and continuous, whether and how it encourages a holistic and co-operative approach to the delivery of care, its cost-effectiveness, the respect for the care provider it expresses, and the degree of its emphasis on the promotion of health and the prevention of disease and injury. These issues are based both on the key recommendations of recent British Columbia government reports and on the claims made for Managed Care by its advocates in the United States. The researchers also asked, in more open-ended fashion, about problems with health care and its reform. This involved questions on deskilling, work intensification, the reinforcement of a medical model that aggressively treats body parts rather than caring for whole persons, and the shifting of decision-making authority from health professionals working with their patients to distant administrators using formulas for approving diagnostic and treatment procedures.

More generally, discussion in the interviews delved into how 'reform' has been experienced in health care, as revealed for instance by the work histories of the participating nurses, by their ongoing learning activities, by their perspectives on changing technologies and divisions of labour, by their assessments of the its implications for the principles of the *Canada Health Act*, and by the concerns they expressed about passing on the traditions and often tacit knowledge of nursing.

The Qualitative Approach

In order to get at how nurses really provide health care in practice, as distinct from any official line about how it is designed to be provided, the interviews were conducted with the use of a semi-structured schedule of questions. The research team wanted certain topics addressed in each interview. It did not however insist that the topics be covered in any particular order. And it wanted to ensure that the nurses as well as the researchers had a say in how the topics were defined, in how much emphasis was placed on each topic, and in whether and how topics were connected to each other.

In other words, because a semi-structured approach was used, decisions concerning what is important about health care were reached, implicitly or explicitly, by means of extended and quite free-wheeling conversations among the researchers and the nurses. These decisions were not imposed unilaterally and in advance by the researchers.

The semi-structured approach also allowed the researchers, and indeed the nurses as well, to probe deeply into what emerged as the particularly significant topics, exploring possible meanings and interpretations of the points raised in conversation. In this way, not only could shared understandings be reached, but also more persistent ambiguities and issues of vagueness could be identified. The clarifications achieved through dialogue are especially important to researchers from Ontario seeking to understand B.C. realities. There is of course much that is the same in how terms get used across the country. But there are also subtle differences in usage. Failure to recognize and compensate for differences in usage can add appreciably to the difficulties all researchers face in their efforts to determine the meanings attached to words.

The reasons for conducting group interviews are straightforward. The intervention of one participant often stimulates the thinking of others, enabling them to view the issue at hand in new ways and helping them to recall events from the recesses of their memories. As previously noted, the dialogue among participants can lead to the clarification of issues. A group process helps to maintain the focus on issues rather than on individuals. And, finally, the presence of co-workers can serve to enhance the accuracy of what is said. False impressions and partial knowledge can be corrected and the temptation to tell the researchers what participants perceive that they want to hear, rather than what actually happened, is reduced.

The Involvement of the Researchers

The research team brings together individuals with considerable experience in the use of qualitative data, and more particularly the use of semi-structured interviews. In 1983, Pat Armstrong and Hugh Armstrong combined data from semi-structured interviews with 65 working class women across Canada and official labour force statistics to produce *A Working Majority: What Women Must Do for Pay.*[1] Out of that study came an article in which they elaborated on the inadequacies of an exclusive reliance on quantitative approaches.[2] In 1990, Jerry P. White published *Hospital Strike: Women, Unions, and Public Sector Conflict*, a case study that involved "seeking rather than testing" and that relied heavily on semi-structured interviews.[3]

The research team itself first came together to conduct and analyze the semi-structured group interviews with hospital workers for the report entitled "Voices from the Ward". This report, which documented deterioration in the quality of care offered by Ontario hospitals as a result of funding cuts, provoked much public discussion. One outcome was that it was reprinted as the centrepiece of a book by team members entitled *Take Care: Warning Signals for Canada's Health System.*[4] One of the other chapters in this volume was a discussion of the team's interview methodology.

The report also prompted hundreds of calls from patients and the families and friends of patients who wanted to add their stories to the "Voices". In response, the report's union sponsor set up a phone hotline with a 1-800 number, and additional hundreds of long, semi-structured interviews were conducted. The resulting report, "When Patients Don't Matter", was also reprinted as a book chapter, in *Medical Alert: New Work Organizations in Health Care.*[5] The report of another team research project based on semi-structured group interviews is also reprinted in this volume. "The Promise and the Price" examines the implementation in health care settings of Total Quality Management and related work reorganization schemes.

The strength of all these research efforts lies in bringing together the experiences, perspectives and insights of health sector workers with the analytical tools of social science as employed by researchers who are familiar with the health sector. Alone, neither the contributions of the providers nor those of the researchers could produce the depth of understanding that results from sustained conversations among providers and researchers in semi-structured group interview settings.

The exchanges in the settings, however fruitful, are of course not the end of the matter. It remains for the researchers to organize the material into a coherent, theoretically informed analysis. In the case of this study, the double set of tapes was transformed into a set of transcripts which were read and discussed by the entire team. Pat Armstrong then produced a draft report, which became the subject of further team discussions and which resulted in the current draft. This draft was sent back to the BCNU for comments. Although responsibility for the content of the report rests entirely with the research team, feedback has been sought from those interviewed and from their co-workers in order both to confirm that the basic thrust and tone of the report are accurate and to identify emphases and formulations that merit re-examination.

In past projects, the research team has obtained this feedback by circulating the draft to participants in a conference of health sector workers, where it was then discussed. Given the distances involved between British Columbia nurses and Ontario researchers, face-to-face feedback has not been feasible this time round, but every effort has been made to secure feedback in other ways.

Notes

[1] Pat Armstrong and Hugh Armstrong, *A Working Majority: What Women Must Do for Pay*. Ottawa: Supply and Services Canada for the Canadian Advisory Council on the Status of Women, 1983.

[2] Pat Armstrong and Hugh Armstrong, "Beyond Numbers: Problems with Quantitative Data" reprinted as pp. 54-79 in Greta Hoffman Nemiroff (ed.), *Women and Men: Interdisciplinary Readings on Gender*. Toronto: Fitzhenry and Whiteside, 1987.

[3] Jerry P. White, *Hospital Strike: Women, Unions, and Public Sector Conflict*. Toronto: Thompson Educational Publishing, 1990.

[4] Pat Armstrong et al., *Take Care: Warning Signals for Canada's Health System*. Toronto: Garamond Press, 1994.

[5] Pat Armstrong et al., *Medical Alert: New Work Organizations in Health Care*. Toronto: Garamond Press, 1997.

Appendix B
Information and Consent Form
Managed Care vs Managing Care Study

The purpose of this comparative study is to examine the experiences and views of those who work in the health care sector on the management of care in the United States and Canada. Care is rapidly changing in both countries, and management practices originating largely in the U.S. are spreading north and south of the border. The impacts of these practices on the quality of care, on access to care and on cost-effectiveness need to be assessed. In the view of our research team, which consists of five individuals from Ontario universities joined by the director of research for a nurses association, there is no more vital source of information than those who directly provide the care under these changing conditions. We hope you'll agree.

As part of the study, Pat Armstrong and Hugh Armstrong of Carleton University in Ottawa and conducting taped, two-hour group interviews with British Columbia nurses. The groups have been set up by the British Columbia Nurses Union, which is a sponsor of the study but which has no further involvement in how it is conducted. Through a similar arrangement with the California Nurses Association, we conducted interviews in California last month.

Your voluntary participation in one of these group interviews is requested. Should you agree, you will retain the right to refuse to answer any of the interview questions for whatever reason, and to withdraw from the study at any time. The tapes, transcripts and interviewer notes from the interviews will be available only to the research team and those directly employed by it. No oral or written report on the study will contain your name, that of your employer or any other identifying information.

The results of the study will be made available to the BCNU for distribution to its members and others as it sees fit. The research team will also prepare for academic publication a report or reports on the study. For further information about the study, you may contact:

> Dr. Hugh Armstrong
> School of Social Work
> Carleton University
> Ottawa ON Canada K1S 5B6
> Phone: (613) 520-2600, ext. 1890
> e-mail: harmstro@ccs.carleton.ca

I, _____ (please print), having read the above description of the "Managed Care vs Managing Care" study and having received satisfactory answers to my questions about it, hereby indicate my willingness to participate in it.

For the research team	Signature	Date

Notes

[1] Organization for Economic Co-operation and Development, *The Reform of Health Care: A Comparative Analysis of Seven OECD Countries* (Paris: OECD, 1992), 7.

[2] OECD, 1992, 7.

[3] Ibid.

[4] Bengt Jönsson, "Making Sense of Health Care Reform," in OECD, *Health Care Reform: The Will to Change* (Paris: OECD, 1996), 38.

[5] Douglas E. Angus, "A Great Canadian Prescription: Take Two Commissioned Studies and Call Me in the Morning," in *Restructuring Canada's Health Services System: How Do We Get There from Here?*, ed. Raisa B. Deber and Gail G. Thompson (Toronto: University of Toronto Press, 1992), 57.

[6] British Columbia Royal Commission on Health Care and Costs, *Closer to Home: Summary of the Report* (Victoria: Crown Publications, 1991), 15.

[7] OECD, 1992, 15.

[8] National Forum on Health, *Health and Health Care Issues: Summaries of Papers Commissioned by the National Forum on Health* (Ottawa: Ministry of Public Works and Government Services Canada, February 1997) 32.

[9] Stephen M. Shortell, Robin R. Gillies, David A. Anderson, Karen Morgan Erickson and John B. Mitchell, *Remaking Health Care in America* (San Francisco: Jossey-Bass, 1996), xv.

[10] National Forum on Health, *Health and Health Care Issues*, 32.

[11] Troyen A. Brennan and Donald M. Berwick, *New Rules: Regulation, Markets and the Quality of American Health Care* (San Francisco: Jossey-Bass, 1996) 316.

[12] National Forum on Health, *Health and Health Care Issues*, 35.

[13] Ibid.

[14] British Columbia Royal Commission on Health Care and Costs, *Closer to Home*, 3.

[15] In 1997, there were 229,990 RNs employed in Canada. See CIHI Homepage Registered Nurses Working Part...Community-Based Care, 1997 Figures. www.cihi.CA/facts/rn.htm, 06/08/98, Tables 1 and 3.

[16] Details on the methodology are provided in the Appendix to this report.

[17] See Theresa Boyle, "Bringing Nurses Home," *Toronto Star* (14 February 1999), A6, using 1992–97 data from CIHI. The growth in the number of nurses is not, however, reflected in a growth in the number of nursing hours. A shift from full-time to part-time and casual employment, experienced by all union and non-contract groups in the acute-care sector in BC, appears to be affecting RNs disproportionately. See Healthcare Labour Adjustment Agency, *Bulletin* 2:3 (28 June 1996), which reports that from Dec. 1992 to Dec. 1995, BCNU members lost 1,126 full-time jobs, or 47.3% of the total full-time job loss, despite having only 34% of the total hours in 1992. The CIHI numbers likely can be explained by the growth in part-time and casual hours for BCNU members during this and subsequent periods (up 1.6% and 12.7%, respectively, for 1992–95).

[18] Chapters 1 and 2 are revised versions of a paper prepared for the Working Group on Women and Health Reform, Health Canada, 1999.

[19] Judi Coburn, "'I See and Am Silent': A Short History of Nursing in Ontario, 1850–1930," in *Health and Canadian Society*, 2nd edition, ed. David Coburn, Carl D'Arcy, George M. Torrance and Peter New (Markham: Fitzhenry and Whiteside, 1987), 442.

[20] Abraham Flexner, *Medical Education in the United States and Canada* (New York: Arno, 1972).

[21] Malcolm Taylor, *Health Insurance and Canadian Public Policy*, 2nd edition (Montréal: McGill-Queen's University Press, 1987), 17.

[22] See Ann Pederson, Michel O'Neill and Irving Rootman, eds., *Health Promotion in Canada: Provincial, National and International Perspectives* (Toronto: W.B. Saunders, 1994).

[23] Taylor, 1987, 2.

[24] Sylvia Bashevkin, *Women on the Defensive: Living Through Conservative Times* (Toronto: University of Toronto Press, 1998), 19.

[25] Advisory Committee on Reconstruction, *Post-War Problems of Women: Final Report of the Subcommittee* (Ottawa: King's Printer, 1944).

[26] Mica Panic, "The Bretton Woods System: Concept and Practice" in *The Global Economy*, ed. Jonathan Michie and John Grieve Smith (Oxford: Oxford University Press, 1995), 38.

[27] Panic, 1995, 38.

[28] Bashevkin, 1998, 19.

[29] Panic, 1995, 38.

[30] The Constitution of WHO as set out in Meri Koivusalo and Eeva Ollila, *Making a Healthy World: Agencies, Actors & Policies in International Health* (London: Zed Books, 1997), 7. This book provides an excellent summary of the development and responsibilities of various international organizations involved in health issues.

[31] Organization for Economic Co-operation and Development, *The Future of Female Dominated Occupations* (Paris: OECD, 1998), 131.

[32] World Health Organization, *The World Health Report 1998* (Geneva: WHO, 1998), 11.

[33] See Jane Stein, *Empowerment and Women's Health: Theory, Methods and Practice* (London: Zed Books, 1997).

[34] See OECD, 1998, for data on the growth of nursing work. While there are variations in terms of both growth and the female domination of the occupation, the number of jobs increased significantly between 1985 and 1995, and the overwhelming majority of nurses in all countries surveyed were women.

[35] Dominion Bureau of Statistics, *Canada 1957* (Ottawa: Queen's Printer, 1957), 267.

[36] Taylor, 1987, 111.

[37] Ibid., 114.

[38] Leonard Marsh, *Report on Social Security for Canada 1943* (Toronto: University of Toronto Press, 1975), 9–10.

[39] Quoted in Taylor, 1987, 50.

[40] Ibid., 375.

[41] National Forum on Health, "Striking a Balance Working Group Synthesis Report," in *Canada Health Action: Building on the Legacy*. Volume II, *Synthesis Reports and Issues Papers* (Ottawa: Minister of Public Works and Government, 1997), 16.

[42] Josephine Rekart, *Public Funds, Private Provision* (Vancouver: University of British Columbia Press, 1993).

[43] Shelagh Day and Gwen Brodsky, *Women and the Equality Deficit* (Ottawa: Status of Women Canada, 1998), 17.

[44] Taylor, 1987, 344–55.

[45] James Struthers, "Reluctant Partners. State Regulation of Private Nursing Homes in Ontario, 1941–72,"in *The Welfare State in Canada: Past, Present and Future*, ed. Raymond B. Blake, Penny E. Bryden and J. Frank Strain (Toronto: Irwin, 1997).

[46] Quoted in Struthers, 1997, 177.

[47] Ibid., 178–79.

[48] Ibid., 181.

[49] Struthers, 1997, 186.

[50] Frederic Lesemann, *Services and Circuses* (Montréal: Black Rose Books, 1984), 244.

[51] Marc Renaud, "Reform or Illusion? An Analysis of the Quebec State Intervention in Health," in *Health and Canadian Society*, 2nd edition, ed. David Coburn, Carl D'Arcy, George Torrance and Peter New (Markham: Fitzhenry and Whiteside, 1987).

[52] David Naylor, *Public Payment, Private Practice* (Montréal: McGill-Queen's University Press, 1986).

[53] Philip Enterline, Allison McDonald, J. Corbett McDonald and Nicholas Steinmetz, "The Distribution of Medical Services Before and After 'Free' Medicare," *Medical Care* 11, no. 4 (July/August 1973): 269–86.

[54] Dominion Bureau of Statistics, *Labour Force, Occupation and Industry Trends* (Ottawa: Minister of Trade and Commerce, 1966), Table 12B.

[55] Statistics Canada, *91 Census, Industry and Class of Worker* (Ottawa: Minister of Industry, Science and Technology, 1993), Table 1 (Cat. no. 93-326).

[56] See Pat Armstrong, Jacqueline Choiniere and Elaine Day, *Vital Signs: Nursing in Transition*, Toronto: Garamond Press, 1993; and Pat Armstrong, "Professions, Unions or What? Learning from Nurses," in *Women Challenging Unions: Feminism, Democracy, and Militancy*, ed. Linda Briskin and Patricia McDermott (Toronto: University of Toronto Press, 1993).

[57] See, for example, Nancy Kleiber and Linda Light, *Caring for Ourselves: An Alternative Structure for Health Care* (Vancouver: BC Public Health, 1978); Kathleen McDonnell and Mariana Valverde, *The Health Sharing Book* (Toronto: Women's Press, 1985); and Montréal Women's Press, *The Birth Control Handbook* (Montréal: Montréal Women's Press, 1968).

[58] Carol Bacchi, *Same/Difference* (Sydney: Allen and Unwin, 1990).

[59] See, for example, Sandra Harding, *The Science Question in Feminism* (Ithaca: Cornell University Press, 1986); and *Whose Science? Whose Knowledge? Thinking from Women's Lives* (Ithaca: Cornell University Press, 1991).

[60] Susan Sherwin, "Introduction," in Susan Sherwin (coordinator), *The Politics of Women's Health: Exploring Agency and Autonomy* (Philadelphia: Temple University Press, 1998), 12.

[61] Astrid Brousselle, "Controlling Health Expenditures: What Matters," in National Forum on Health, *Health Care Systems in Canada and Elsewhere* (Sainte-Foy: Editions MultiMondes, 1998), 52.

[62] See B. Singh Bolaria and Rosemary Bolaria, eds., *Racial Minorities in Medicine and Health* (Halifax: Fernwood, 1994).

[63] John Shields and B. Mitchell Evans, *Shrinking the State: Globalization and Public Administration "Reform"* (Halifax: Fernwood, 1998), 11.

[64] Bashevkin, 1998, 19.

[65] Michael Mendelson, *The Capitalist Models: Where They Came from and Where They May Go* (Ottawa: Caledon Institute of Social Policy, 1997).

[66] Alan Walker, quoted in Brendan Martin, *In the Public Interest? Privatization and Public Sector Reform* (London: Zed Books, 1993), 46.

[67] Martin, 1993, 48.

[68] Bashevkin, 1998, 22.

[69] Shields and Evans, 1998, 17.

[70] Paul Starr, *The Limits of Privatization* (Washington: Economic Policy Institute, 1987), 1.

[71] Ian Taylor, quoted in Martin, 1993, 48.

[72] Bashevkin, 1998, 28.

[73] Heather Gibb, *Gender Front and Centre* (Ottawa: North-South Institute, 1997), 2.

[74] See Gibb, 1997, and Pamela Sparr, ed., *Mortgaging Women's Lives: Feminist Critiques of Structural Adjustment* (London: Zed Books, 1994).

[75] Organization for Economic Co-operation and Development, *Governance in Transition: Public Management Reforms in OECD Countries* (Paris: OECD, 1995), 19.

[76] David Osborne and Ted Gaebler, *Reinventing Government: How the Entrepreneurial Spirit is Transforming the Public Sector* (New York: Plume, 1992), 281.

[77] Ibid., 282.

[78] Jon Pierre, "The Marketization of the State: Citizens, Consumers, and the Emergence of the Public Market," in *Governance in a Changing Environment*, ed. B. Guy Peters and Donald J. Savoie (Montréal: McGill-Queen's University Press, 1995), 56.

[79] See, for example, Susan Boyd, ed., *Challenging the Public/Private Divide: Feminism, Law and Public Policy* (Toronto: University of Toronto Press, 1997); and Janine Brodie, ed., *Women and Canadian Public Policy* (Toronto: Harcourt Brace, 1996).

[80] Susan Sherwin, *No Longer Patient: Feminist Ethics and Health Care* (Philadelphia: Temple University Press, 1992), 6.

[81] See, for example, Kathleen McDonnell, ed., *Adverse Effects: Women and the Pharmaceutical Industry* (Toronto: Women's Press, 1986); Christine Overall, *Human Reproduction: Principles, Practices and Policies* (Toronto: Oxford, 1993); and Jan Rehner, *Infertility: Old Myths, New Meanings* (Toronto: Second Story Press, 1989).

[82] Rosalind Pollack Petchesky, "From Population Control to Reproductive Rights: Feminist Fault Lines," *Reproductive Health Matters* 6 (November 1995): 152.

[83] Ibid.

[84] Ibid., 156.

[85] Ibid., 157.

[86] Ibid.

[87] Rekart, 1993.

[88] See Harvey Simmons, *Unbalanced: Mental Health Policy in Ontario, 1930–1989* (Toronto: Wall and Thompson, 1990).

[89] Pat Armstrong, "Unraveling the Safety Net: Transformations in Health Care and Their Impact on Women," in Janine Brodie, ed., *Women and Canadian Public Policy* (Toronto: Harcourt Brace, 1996).

[90] Trevor Hancock, "Health Promotion in Canada: Did We Win the Battle But Lose the War?," in Ann Pederson, Michel O'Neill and Irving Rootman, eds., *Health Promotion in Canada* (Toronto: W.B. Saunders, 1994), 365.

[91] See Mary Ruggie, *Realignments in the Welfare State: Health Policy in the United States, Britain, and Canada* (New York: Columbia University Press, 1996), chapter 1.

[92] OECD, 1995, 19.

[93] See, for example, Diane Sainsbury, *Gender, Equality and Welfare States* (Cambridge: Cambridge University Press, 1996); and Ruggie, 1996.

[94] H. Mimoto and P. Cross, "The Growth of the Federal Debt," *The Canadian Economic Observer* (June 1991): 1.

[95] See Pat Armstrong and Hugh Armstrong, *Universal Health Care: What the United States Can Learn from Canada* (New York: New Press, 1998), Table 6.5.

[96] Shields and Evans, 1998, 23.

[97] OECD, 1996, 7.

[98] Brousselle, 1998, 52.

[99] Harold Chorney, "Debts, Deficits and Full Employment," in *States Against Markets: The Limits of Globalization*, ed. Robert Boyer and Daniel Drache (London: Routledge, 1996), 358.

[100] See Sainsbury, 1996.

[101] Ake Blomqvist and David M. Brown, eds., *Limits to Care: Reforming Canada's Health System in an Age of Restraint* (Toronto: C.D. Howe Institute, 1994).

[102] Carmen Lawrence, "Opening Statement," OECD, 1996, 12.

[103] Struthers, 1997, 174 and 196.

[104] OECD, 1996, 11.

[105] Henry Aaron, "Thinking About Health Care Financing: Some Propositions," in OECD, 1996, 52.

[106] Ibid.

[107] OECD, 1996, 7.

[108] Robert G. Evans, Morris L. Barer and Theodore R. Marmor, *Why Are Some People Healthy and Others Not? The Determinants of Health of Populations* (New York: Aldine De Gruyter, 1994), xii.

[109] Jan Rehner, *Infertility: Old Myths, New Meanings* (Toronto: Second Story Press, 1989).

[110] Brian Abel-Smith, "The Escalation of Health Care Costs: How Did We Get There?" in OECD, 1996, 27.

[111] See, for example, Pat Armstrong, "Closer to Home: More Work for Mother," in Pat Armstrong et al., *Take Care: Warning Signals for Canada's Health System* (Toronto: Garamond Press, 1994); Jane Aronson and Sheila Neysmith, "The Retreat of the State and Long-Term Provisions: Implications for Frail Elderly People, Unpaid Family Carers and Paid Home Care Workers," *Studies in Political Economy* 53 (Summer 1997): 37–66; Nina Chappell, "Implications of Shifting Health Care Policy for Care-Givers in Canada," *Journal of Aging and Social Policy* 51, no. ½ (1993): 39–55; and Nona Glazer, *Women's Paid and Unpaid Labor: The Work Transfer in Health Care and Retailing* (Philadelphia: Temple University Press, 1993).

[112] Monique Jérôme-Forget and Claude E. Forget, *Who Is the Master? A Blueprint for Canadian Health Care Reform* (Montréal: Institute for Research on Public Policy, 1998), 15.

[113] Koivusalo and Ollila, 1997, 3.

[114] Ibid., 18.

[115] See Koivusalo and Ollila, 1997; Joseph l. Scarpaci, ed., *Health Services Privatization in Industrial Societies* (New Brunswick, N.J.: Rutgers University Press, 1989).

[116] Kathy Megyery and Frank Sader, *Facilitating Foreign Participation in Privatization* (Washington: World Bank, 1996), 3.

[117] Ibid., abstract.

[118] Joyce Nelson, "Dr. Rockefeller Will See You Now," *Canadian Forum* (January/February 1995): 7. See also Colleen Fuller, *Caring for Profit* (Ottawa: Canadian Centre for Policy Alternatives, 1991); and Mark A. Peterson, "Introduction: Health Care Into the Next Century," *Journal of Health Politics, Policy and the Law* 22, no. 2 (April 1997): 299.

[119] Deanna Bellandi, "Health Care Industry Gets Clean Bill of Health," *Modern Health Care* (March 16, 1998): 68.

[120] Kenneth E. Thorpe, "The Health System in Transition: Care, Cost and Coverage," *Journal of Health Politics, Policy and the Law* 22, no. 2 (April 1997): 343.

[121] Peterson, 1997, 299.

[122] Werner Christie, "Keynote Address," in OECD, 1996, 14.

[123] OECD, 1992, 10.

[124] Jönsson, 1996, 8.

[125] Jérôme-Forget and Forget, 1998, 12.

[126] Christie, 1996, 14.

[127] David U. Himmelstein and Steffie Woolhandler, *The National Health Program Book* (Monroe, ME: Common Courage Press, 1994).

[128] Raisa Deber et al., "The Public-Private Mix in Health Care," in National Forum on Health, *Health Care Systems in Canada and Elsewhere* (Sainte-Foy: Editions MultiMondes, 1998).

[129] Jönsson, 1996, 39.

[130] Ibid.

[131] Starr, 1987, 5.

[132] Struthers, 1997.

[133] Starr, 1987, 7.

[134] Rekart, 1993.

[135] Pat Armstrong et al., *Medical Alert: New Work Organizations in Health Care* (Toronto: Garamond Press, 1997).

[136] Glazer, 1993; Deber et al., 1998.

[137] Starr, 1978, 7.

[138] Robert Evans et al., "Who are the Zombies and What Do They Want?," (Toronto: Ontario Premier's Council on Health, Well-Being, and Social Justice, June 1994).

[139] See Morris Barer, Vanda Bhatia, Greg Stoddart and Robert Evans, "The Remarkable Tenacity of User Charges" (Toronto: Ontario Premier's Council on Health, Well-Being and Social Justice, 1994).

[140] Greg Stoddart, Morris Barer, Robert Evans and Vanda Bhatia, "Why Not User Charges? The Real Issues" (Toronto: Ontario Premier's Council on Health, Well-Being and Social Justice, 1993), 7.

[141] Carolyn A. DeCosta and Marni D. Brownell, "Private Health Care in Canada: Savior or Siren," *Public Health Reports* 112 (July/August 1997): 299–305.

[142] Deber and Swan, 1998, 335.

[143] Christie, 1996, 13

[144] Lee N. Newcomer, MD, Vice-President, Health Services Operations, United Health Care Corporation, as quoted by Working Group on Health Services Utilization, "When Less Is Better: Using Canada's Hospitals Efficiently," a paper written for the June 1994 Conference of Federal/Provincial/Territorial Deputy Ministers of Health, 16.

[145] Deborah Stone, *Policy Paradox: The Art of Political Decision Making*, (New York: W.W. Norton, 1997)

[146] Leslie Laurence and Beth Weinhouse, *Outrageous Practices: How Gender Bias Threatens Women's Health* (New Brunswick, N.J.: Rutgers University Press, 1997), 5.

[147] Ann Oakley, "Who's Afraid of the Randomized Controlled Trial? Some Dilemmas of the Scientific Method and 'Good' Research Practice," in *Women's Health Counts*, ed. Helen Robert (London: Routledge, 1990), 167–94.

[148] See, for example, Pat Armstrong, "Women and Health: Challenges and Changes," in *Feminist Issues: Race, Class and Sexuality*, ed. Nancy Mandell (Scarborough: Prentice- Hall, 1998), 249–66; Kary L. Moss, *Man-Made Medicine: Women's Health, Public Policy and Reform* (Durham: Duke University Press, 1996); and Jane Stein, *Empowerment and Women's Health Theory, Methods and Practice* (London: Zed Books, 1997). *The Politics of Women's Health: Exploring Agency and Autonomy*, coordinated by Susan Sherwin, is particularly valuable on these issues.

[149] Julie A. Nelson, *Feminism, Objectivity and Economics*, (London: Routledge, 1996), 30.

[150] Wendy Mitchinson, "Agency, Diversity, and Constraints: Women and Their Physicians, Canada 1850–1950,"in Sherwin, 1998, 136 and 138.

[151] Gene Swimmer, "An Introduction to Life Under the Knife," in *How Ottawa Spends: Life Under the Knife*, ed. Gene Swimmer (Ottawa: Carleton University Press, 1996-97), 1.

[152] Ibid.

[153] 1995 budget speech by Finance Minister Paul Martin, February 27, 1995.

[154] Quoted in Gilles Paquet and Robert Shepherd, "The Program Review Process: A Deconstruction," in Swimmer, 1996, 25.

[155] Ibid.

[156] Judy D'Arcy, "A Futuristic Nightmare," *Healthsharing* (Fall 1988): 19.

[157] Monique Bégin, "Free Trade Will Destroy Our Precious Medicare," *The Toronto Star* (October 28, 1988).

[158] Colleen Fuller, "A Matter of Life and Death: NAFTA and Medicare," *Canadian Forum* (October 1993): 14–19.

[159] Janet Maher, "Healthcare in Crisis," *Healthsharing* 14, no. 2 (1993): 13.

[160] See Barrie McKenna, "Provinces Take Steps to Shield Health Care," *The Globe and Mail* (March 26, 1996): B1; and Colleen Fuller, "The Conspiracy to Implement NAFTA and End Medicare," *Canadian Perspectives* (Autumn 1995): 11.

[161] Maher, 1993.

[162] Bryan Schwartz, "NAFTA Reservations in the Areas of Health Care," opinion, Winnipeg. File no. 24703 (March 4, 1996): 1.

[163] Ibid.

[164] Mel Clark, "Chrétien Government Killing Medicare System It Promised to Save," *CCPA Monitor* 5, no. 9 (March 1999): 11.

[165] Marjorie Cohen, *Free Trade and the Future of Women's Work: Manufacturing and Service Industries* (Toronto: Garamond Press, 1987).

[166] Tony Clarke and Maude Barlow, *MAI. Round 2* (Toronto: Stoddart, 1998), 11.

[167] See Day and Brodsky, 1998.

[168] Ernest B. Akyeampong, "The Rise of Unionization Among Women," *Perspectives on Labour and Income* 10, no. 4 (Winter 1998): 31.

[169] Ibid, 34.

[170] Canadian Council on Social Development, *Public Sector Downsizing: The Impact on Job Quality in Canada* (Ottawa: CCSD, 1997). It should be noted that there are somewhat different definitions used for private and public sector in the reports by Akyeampong and the CCSD. This is also the case even within the reports themselves. As a result, the data are not strictly comparable. Nonetheless, the patterns are clear.

[171] Akyeampong, 1998, Appendix.

[172] *A Framework to Improve the Social Union for Canadians,* an agreement between the Government of Canada and the governments of the provinces and the territories (February 4, 1999).

[173] For summaries of the various provincial reports, see Angus, 1992; and Raisa Deber, Sharmila Mhatre and G. Ross Baker, "A Review of Provincial Initiatives," in Blomqvist and Brown, 1994, 91–124.

[174] Ralph Sutherland and Jane Fulton, *Spending Smarter and Spending Less: Policies and Partnerships for Health Care in Canada* (Ottawa: Canadian Hospital Association Press, 1994).

[175] John L. Dorland and S. Mathwin Davis, eds., *How Many Roads...? Regionalization & Decentralization in Health Care* (Kingston: Queen's School of Policy Studies, 1996).

[176] See British Columbia Royal Commission on Health Care and Costs, *Closer to Home: A Summary Report* (Victoria: BC Royal Commission on Health Care, 1991).

[177] Armstrong et al., 1997.

[178] Eva Ryten, *A Statistical Picture of the Past, Present and Future of Registered Nurses in Canada* (Ottawa: Canadian Nurses Association, 1997), Table 3.

[179] Laura Sky, *Lean and Mean Health Care: The Creation of the Generic Worker and the Deregulation of Health Care*. Working Paper 95-3, Health Research Project (Ontario Federation of Labour, June 1995).

[180] Jerry White, *Hospital Strike: Women, Unions, and Public Sector Conflict* (Toronto: Thompson, 1990).

[181] Centre for Health Economics and Policy Analysis, "*The Party of the First Part...*" *Contracting in Health Care* (Hamilton: CHEPA, 1997).

[182] Alan Maynard, "United Kingdom," in Dorland and Davis, 1996, 63.

[183] Frederic Lesemann and Daphne Nahmiash, "Home-Based Care in Canada and Quebec," in *Home-Based Care: The Elderly, the Family and the Welfare State: An International Comparison*, ed. Frederic Lesemann and Claude Martin (Ottawa: University of Ottawa Press, 1993), 96.

[184] Jane Aronson and Sheila Neysmith, "The Work of Visiting Homemakers in the Context of Cost Cutting in Long Term Care," *Canadian Journal of Public Health* 87, no. 6 (1996): 422–25.

[185] Sheila Neysmith and Jane Aronson, "Home Care Workers Discuss Their Work: The Skills Required to 'Use Your Common Sense'," *Journal of Aging Studies* 10, no. 1 (1996): 1–14.

[186] Sheila Neysmith and Jane Aronson, "Working Conditions in Home Care: Negotiating Race and Class Boundaries in Gendered Work," *International Journal of Health Services* 27, no.3 (1997): 479–99.

[187] Evelyn Shapiro, *The Cost of Privatization: A Case Study of Manitoba* (Ottawa: Canadian Centre for Policy Alternatives, 1997).

[188] See, for example, Linda McLeod, *Wife Battering in Canada: The Vicious Circle* (Ottawa: Canadian Advisory Council on the Status of Women, 1980); and N. Chappell, I. Strain and A. Blandford, *Aging and Health Care: A Social Perspective* (Toronto: Holt, Rinehart and Winston, 1986).

[189] Sylvie Jutras and Frances Veilleux, "Informal Caregiving: Correlates of Perceived Burden," *Canadian Journal on Aging* 10, no.1 (1991): 50.

[190] Health Canada, *Health Reform Data Base Overview by Province, 1998–99* (Ottawa: Health Canada, 1999).

[191] Quoted in Lesemann, 1984, 145.

[192] *Report* of the Eastman Commission of Inquiry on the Pharmaceutical Industry (Ottawa: Supply and Services Canada, 1985).

[193] Canadian Drug Manufacturers' Association, *The Review of Bill C-91* (North York: Canadian Drug Manufacturers' Association, nd [1998?]).

[194] National Forum on Health, "Directions for a Pharmaceutical Policy in Canada," in *Canada Health Action: Building on the Legacy*, 1997, 5.

[195] Ibid., 4.

[196] Statistics Canada, *Earnings of Women and Men, 1995* (Ottawa: Ministry of Industry, 1997), Table 2.

[197] Michael Fitz-James, "Happy Birthday, Reference-Based Pricing," *Canadian Healthcare Manager* 3, no. 6 (October/November 1996): 12.

[198] National Forum on Health, "Directions for a Pharmaceutical Policy," 1997, 7.

[199] Ibid., 8.

[200] Don De Vortez and Samuel A. Laryea, *Canadian Human Capital Transfers: The United States and Beyond* (Toronto: C.D. Howe Institute, October 1998), 9.

[201] Ibid., Table 5.

[202] Terry Wotherspoon, "Immigration, Gender and Professional Labour: State Regulation of Nursing and Teaching." Paper presented to the CSAA 25th Annual Meeting, Victoria, May 1990.

[203] Health Canada, *Shared Responsibilities: Shared Vision* (Ottawa: Health Canada, 1998).

[204] William Walker, "PM Forging Ahead on Health Accord," *The Toronto Star* (27 January 1999): A7.

205 Ann McIlroy, "Canadians' Medical Data Should Be On Computer, Panel Says," *The Globe and Mail* (4 February, 1999): A4.

206 "'Report Cards' Proposed for Health-Care Services," *The Toronto Star* (4 February 1999): A6.

207 Advisory Council on Health Infostructure, *Canada Health Infoway: Paths to Better Health. Final Report* (Ottawa: Ministry of Public Works and Government Services, 1999).

208 Canadian Institute for Health Information, "A Partnership Invitation," nd, np.

209 "'Report Cards'," *The Toronto Star*, A6.

210 *Framework to Improve the Social Union*, 2.

211 Sherwin, 1998, 24.

212 Ibid.

213 Health and Welfare Canada, *Privatization in the Canadian Health Care System: Assertions, Evidence, Ideology and Options* (Ottawa: Health and Welfare Canada, 1985), 68.

214 Robert G. Evans, "Going for the Gold: The Redistribution Agenda behind Market-Based Health Care Reform," *Journal of Health Politics, Policy and Law* 22, no. 2 (April 1997): 428.

215 Ibid.

216 National Forum on Health, *Health and Health Care Issues*, 35

217 National Forum on Health, *Health and Health Care Issues*.

218 Ibid., 35

219 British Columbia Royal Commission on Health Care and Costs, *Closer to Home*, 7.

220 British Columbia Ministry of Health and Ministry Responsible for Seniors, *A Guide to Developing Community Health Councils and Regional Health Boards*, Version 1: Meeting the Challenge for a Healthy Society (Victoria: Ministry of Health, May 1993), 3.

221 British Columbia Ministry of Health and Ministry Responsible for Seniors, *New Directions for a Healthy British Columbia* (Victoria: Ministry of Health, 1993), 15.

222 British Columbia Ministry of Health and Ministry Responsible for Seniors, *New Directions*, 15.

223 Pacific Public Affairs Limited, *"New Directions": Anticipated Changes to the Regional Structure of the Health Care System* (Victoria: March 1993), 1.

224 CUPE Research Department, "Job Security Agreement Negotiated Between the Government of British Columbia and the Health Care Unions" (April 1993), 1.

225 See Warren Caragata, "The High Cost of Healing," *Maclean's* (June 15, 1998): 15; and Barbara Wickens, "When Hospitals Lose Beds," *Maclean's*, (June 15, 1998): 21.

226 British Columbia Royal Commission on Health Care and Costs, *Closer to Home*, 16

227 British Columbia, Office of the Premier, *Session Highlights* (March 18, 1993).

228 This and the subsequent direct quotes that appear without attribution are taken from the group interviews conducted in October 1997 with registered nurses in British Columbia.

229 British Columbia Ministry of Health and Ministry Responsible for Seniors, *A Guide to Developing Community Councils and Regional Health Boards*, 3.

230 Ibid., 5.

231 British Columbia Royal Commission on Health Care and Costs, *Closer to Home*, 14.

232 Ibid., 15

[233] Christie, 1996, 13. Emphasis in original.

[234] National Forum on Health, "Creating a Culture of Evidence-based Decision-Making in Health," in *Canada Health Action: Building on the Legacy*, 1997, 6.

[235] See Chapter 2 in Pat Armstrong and Hugh Armstrong, *Wasting Away: The Undermining of Canadian Health Care* (Toronto: Oxford University Press, 1996).

[236] Cheryl Mattingly and Maureen Hayes Fleming, *Clinical Reasoning: Forms of Inquiry in a Therapeutic Practice* (Philadelphia: F.A. Davis, 1994), 9.

[237] Donald Berwick, Blanton Godfrey and Jane Roessner, *Curing Health Care* (San Francisco: Jossey-Bass, 1990), 41.

[238] Working Group on Health Services Utilization, *When Less is Better: Using Canada's Hospitals Efficiently* (Ottawa: Conference of Federal/Provincial/Territorial Deputy Ministers of Health, 1994), 16.

[239] Bruce Goldfarb, *Health Care Defined* (Baltimore: Williams and Wilkins, 1997), 116.

[240] Brennan and Berwick, *New Rules*, 1996, 313.

[241] Karen Davis, Karen Scott Collins and Cynthia Morris, "Managed Care: Promise and Concerns," *Health Affairs* (Fall 1994).

[242] Linda G. Aiken, Herbert L. Smith and Eileen T. Lake, "Lower Medicare Mortality Among a Set of Hospitals Known for Good Nursing Care," *Medical Care* 32 (1994), no. 8: 771–87; and Abdolmohsin S. Al-Haider and Thomas T.H. Wan, "Modeling Organizational Determinants of Hospital Mortality," *Health Services Research* 26 (1991), no. 3: 303–23.

[243] Gooloo S. Wunderlich, Frank A. Sloan and Carolyne K. Davis, eds., *Nursing Staff in Hospitals and Nursing Homes: Is it Adequate?* (Washington, DC: National Academy Press, 1996).

[244] Ann Pederson, Michel O'Neill and Irving Rootman, eds., "Preface," in *Health Promotion in Canada: Provincial, National and International Perspectives* (Toronto: W.B. Saunders, 1994), 1.

[245] British Columbia Ministry of Health and Ministry Responsible for Seniors, *New Directions*, 12.

[246] Ibid., 7.

[247] Ibid., 17.

[248] See the Whitehall Studies by Michael Marmot et al., for example, M.G. Marmot, Rose G. Shipley and M. Hamilton, "Employment Grade and Coronary Heart Disease in British Civil Servants," *Journal of Epidemiology and Community Health* 32 (1978): 244–49.

[249] For examples of the rich research literature on the implications of standardization in health care reform, see Marc Berg, "Problems and Promises of the Protocol," *Social Science and Medicine* 44, no. 8 (1997): 1081–88; G.S. Belkin, "The Technocratic Wish: Making Sense and Finding Power in the 'Managed' Marketplace," *Journal of Health Politics, Policy and Law* 22, no. 2 (April 1997): 509–26; David Frankford, "Scientism and Economics in the Regulation of Health Care," *Journal of Health Politics, Policy and Law* 19, no. 4 (1994): 773–99; and Susan G. Rappolt, "Clinical Guidelines and the Fate of Medical Autonomy in Ontario," *Social Science and Medicine* 44, no. 7 (1997): 977–87.

Bibliography

Aaron, Henry. 1996. "Thinking About Health Care Financing: Some Propositions." In *Health Reform: The Will To Change*, **Paris: OECD.**

Abel-Smith, Brian. 1996. "The Escalation of Health Care Costs: How Did We Get There?" In OECD.

Advisory Committee on Reconstruction. 1944. *Post-War Problems of Women: Final Report of the Subcommittee.* Ottawa, King's Printer.

Advisory Council on Health Infostructure. 1999. *Canada Health Infoway: Paths to Better Health. Final Report*, Ottawa, Minister of Public Works and Government Services.

Aiken, Linda G., Herbert L. Smith and Eileen T. Lake. 1994, "Lower Medicare Mortality Among a Set of Hospitals Known for Good Nursing Care," *Medical Care*, 32(8):771-87.

Akyeampong, Ernest B. 1998. "The Rise of Unionization Among Women." *Perspectives on Labour and Income*, 10(4), Winter:30-41.

Al-Haider, Abdolmohsin S. and Thomas T.H. Wan. 1991, "Modeling Organizational Determinants of Hospital Mortality," *Health Services Research*, 26(3):303-23.

An agreement between the Government of Canada and the Governments of the Provinces and the Territories. A Framework to Improve the Social Union for Canadians, 4 February 1999.

Angus A., Douglas. 1992. " A Great Canadian Prescription: Take Two Commissioned Studies and Call Me in the Morning." In Raisa B. Deber and Gail G. Thompson (eds.), *Restructuring Canada's Health Services System: How Do We Get There From Here?* Toronto: University of Toronto Press.

Armstrong, Pat. 1993. "Professions, Unions or What? Learning from Nurses." In Linda Briskin and Patricia McDermott (eds.). *Women Challenging Unions: Feminism, Democracy, and Militancy*, Toronto: University of Toronto Press.

Armstrong, Pat. 1994. "Closer to Home: More Work for Mother." In Pat Armstrong et al., *Take Care: Warning Signals For Canada's Health System*, Toronto: Garamond.

Armstrong, Pat. 1996. "Unraveling the Safety Net: Transformations in Health Care and Their Impact on Women." In Brodie, Janine (ed.). 1997. *Women and Canadian Public Policy*, Toronto: University of Toronto Press.

Armstrong, Pat. 1998. "Women and Health: Challenges and Changes." In Nancy Mandell (ed.), *Feminist Issues: Race, Class and Sexuality*, Scarborough: Prentice-Hall.

Armstrong, Pat and Hugh Armstrong. 1998. *Universal Health Care: What the United States Can Learn from Canada*, New York: The New Press.

Armstrong, Pat et al. 1997. *Medical Alert: New Work Organizations in Health Care*, Toronto: Garamond.

Armstrong, Pat, Jacqueline Choiniere and Elaine Day. 1993. *Vital Signs: Nursing in Transition*, Toronto: Garamond.

Aronson, Jane and Sheila Neysmith. 1996. "The Work of Visiting Homemakers in the Context of Cost Cutting in Long Term Care", *Canadian Journal of Public Health*, 87(6): 422-5.

Aronson, Jane and Sheila Neysmith. 1997. "The Retreat of the State and Long-Term Provisions: Implications for Frail Elderly People, Unpaid Family Carers and Paid Home Care Workers." *Studies in Political Economy*, 53, Summer: 37-66.

Bacchi, Carol. 1990. *Same/Difference,* Sydney: Allen and Unwin.

Barer, Morris, Vanda Bhatia, Greg Stoddart and Robert Evans. 1994. "The Remarkable Tenacity of User Charges". Toronto: The Ontario Premier's Council on Health, Well-Being and Social Justice.

Basheykin, Sylvia. 1998. *Women on the Defensive: Living Through Conservative Times,* Toronto: University of Toronto Press.

Bégin, Monique. "Free Trade Will Destroy Our Precious Medicare." *The Toronto Star,* 28 October 1988.

Belkin, G.S. 1997. "The Technocratic Wish: Making Sense and Finding Power in the 'Managed' Marketplace," *Journal of Health Politics, Policy and Law,* 22(2):509-26.

Bellandi, Deanna. 1998. "Health Care Industry Gets Clean Bill of Health", *Modern Health Care*, March 16:68-74.

Berg, Marc. 1997. "Problems and Promises of the Protocol," *Social Science and Medicine* 44(8):1081-88.

Blomqvist, Ake and David M. Brown, (eds.). 1994. *Limits to Care: Reforming Canada's Health System in an Age of Restraint,* Toronto: C.D. Howe Institute.

Boyd, Susan (ed.). 1997. *Challenging the Public/Private Divide: Feminism, Law and Public Policy,* Toronto: University of Toronto Press.

Boyle, Theresa. 1999. "Bringing Nurses Home." *Toronto Star,* 14 February:A6.

Brodie, Janine (ed.). 1997. *Women and Canadian Public Policy,* Toronto: University of Toronto Press.

British Columbia. 1993. Ministry of Health and Ministry Responsible for Seniors, *New Directions for a Healthy British Columbia.* Victoria: Ministry of Health, p.15.

British Columbia. 1993. Office of the Premier, *Session Highlights,* March 18.

British Columbia, Ministry of Health and Ministry Responsible for Seniors. 1993. *A Guide to Developing Community Health Councils and Regional Health Boards,* Version 1: Meeting the Challenge for a Healthy Society. Victoria: Ministry of Health, May:3.

British Columbia Royal Commission on Health Care and Costs. 1991. *Closer to Home: A Summary Report,* Victoria: BC Royal Commission on Health Care, Crown Publications.

Bolaria, B. Singh and Rosemary Bolaria (eds.). 1994. *Racial Minorities in Medicine and Health*, Halifax: Fernwood.

Brennan, Troyen A. and Donald M. Berwick. 1996. *New Rules: Regulation, Markets and the Quality of American Health Care,* San Francisco: Jossey-Bass.

Brousselle, Astrid. 1998. "Controlling Health Expenditures: What Matters." In National Forum on Health, *Health Care Systems in Canada and Elsewhere*, Sainte-Foy: Editions MultiMondes.

Canada. 1999. *A Framework to Improve the Social Union for Canadians,* An Agreement between the Government of Canada and Governments of the Provinces and the Territories, 4 February:2.

Canadian Council on Social Development. 1997. *Public Sector Downsizing: The Impact on Job Quality in Canada,* Ottawa: CCSD.

Canadian Drug Manufacturers' Association. 1998. The Review of Bill C-91. North York: The Canadian Drug Manufacturers' Association, n.d.

Canadian Institute for Health Information. "A Partnership Invitation." No date, No Pagination.

Caragata, Warren. 1998. "The High Cost of Healing." *Maclean's,* June 15:15.

Centre for Health Economics and Policy Analysis. 1997. *"The Part of the First Part..." Contracting in Health Care,* Hamilton: CHEPA.

Chappell, Nina. 1993. "Implications of Shifting Health Care Policy for Care-Givers in Canada." *Journal of Aging and Social Policy,* 51(1/2): 39-55.

Chappell, N., I. Strain and A. Blandford. 1986. *Aging and Health Care: A Social Perspective,* Toronto: Holt, Rinehart and Winston.

Chorney, Harold. 1996. "Debts, Deficits and Full Employment." In Robert Boyer and Daniel Drache (eds.), *States Against Markets: The Limits of Globalization,* London: Routledge.

Christie, Werner. 1996. "Keynote Address." In OECD, *Health Reform: The Will to Change,* Paris: OECD.

CIHI Homepage Registered Nurses Working Part...Community-Based Care, 1997 Figures. http://www.cihi.CA/facts/rn.htm, 06/08/98, Table 1 and Table 3.

Clark, Mel. 1999. "Chrétien Government Killing Medicare System It Promised to Save." *CCPA Monitor,* 5(9), March:11.

Clarke, Tony and Maude Barlow. 1998. *MAI. Round 2,* Toronto: Stoddart.

Coburn, Judi. 1987. "'I See and Am Silent': A Short History of Nursing in Ontario, 1850-1930." In David Coburn, Carl D'Arcy, George M. Torrance and Peter New (eds.). *Health and Canadian Society,* 2nd edition. Markham: Fitzhenry and Whiteside.

Cohen, Marjorie. 1987. *Free Trade and the Future of Women's Work: Manufacturing and Service Industries,* Toronto: Garamond.

CUPE Research Department. 1993. "Job Security Agreement Negotiated Between the Government of British Columbia and the Health Care Unions." April, p.1, mimeo.

D'Arcy, Judy. 1988. "A Futuristic Nightmare." *Healthsharing,* Fall.

Day, Shelagh and Gwen Brodsky. 1998. *Women and the Equality Deficit,* Ottawa, Status of Women: Canada.

DeCosta, Carolyn A. and Marni D. Brownell, 1997. "Private Health Care in Canada: Savior or Siren." *Public Health Reports,* Volume 112, July/August.

Deber, Raisa, Sharmila Mhatre and G. Ross Baker. 1994. "A Review of Provincial Initiatives." In *Blomgvist and Brown*.

Deber, Raisa et al. 1998. "The Public-Private Mix in Health Care." In National Forum on Health, *Health Care Systems in Canada and Elsewhere*, Sainte-Foy: Editions MultiMondes.

De Vortez, Don and Samuel A. Laryea. 1998. *Canadian Human Capital Transfers: The United States and Beyond*, Toronto: C.D. Howe Institute, October p. 9.

Dominion Bureau of Statistics. 1957. *Canada 1957*, Ottawa: Queen's Printer.

Dominion Bureau of Statistics. 1966. *Labour Force, Occupation and Industry Trends*, Ottawa: Minister of Trade and Commerce.

Dorland, John L. and S. Mathwin Davis (eds.). 1996. *How Many Roads...? Regionalization & Decentralization in Health Care*. Kingston: Queen's School of Policy Studies.

Enterline, Philip, Allison McDonald, J. Corbett McDonald, and Nicholas Steinmetz. 1973. "The Distribution of Medical Services Before and After 'Free' Medicare." *Medical Care,* 11(4), July/August:269-86.

Evans, Robert G. 1997. "Going For the Gold: The Redistribution Agenda behind Market-Based Health Care Reform", *Journal of Health Politics, Policy and Law*, Volume 23, No. 2, April:428-65.

Evans, Robert G., Morris L. Barer and Theodore R. Marmor. *1994. Why Are Some People Healthy and Others Not? The Determinants of Health Of Populations*, New York: Aldine De Gruyter.

Evans, Robert et al. 1994. "Who are the Zombies and What Do They Want?" Toronto: The Ontario Premier's Council on Health, Well-Being, and Social Justice, Toronto.

Fitz-James, Michael. 1996. "Happy Birthday, Reference-Based Pricing." *Canadian Healthcare Manager,* 3(6):12, October-November.

Flexner, Abraham. 1972. *Medical Education in the United States and Canada*, New York: Arno.

Fuller, Colleen. 1991. *Caring for Profit*, Ottawa: Canadian Centre for Policy Alternatives.

Fuller, Colleen. 1993. "A Matter of Life and Death: NAFTA and Medicare." *Canadian Forum,* October.

Fuller, Colleen. 1995. "The Conspiracy to Implement NAFTA and End Medicare." *Canadian Perspectives,* Autumn:11.

Frankford, David. 1994. "Scientism and Economics in the Regulation of Health Care." *Journal of Health Politics, Policy and Law,* 19(4):773-99.

Gibb, Heather. 1997. *Gender Front and Centre*, Ottawa: North-South Institute, 1997.

Glazer, Nona. 1993. *Women's Paid and Unpaid Labor: The Work Transfer in Health Care and Retailing*, Philadelphia: Temple University Press.

Hancock, Trevor. 1994. Hancock, "Health Promotion in Canada: Did We Win the Battle But Lose the War?" In Ann Pederson, Michel O'Neill and Irving Rootman (eds.), *Health Promotion in Canada*, Toronto: Harcourt Brace.

Harding, Sandra. 1991. *Whose Science? Whose Knowledge? Thinking from Women's Lives*, Ithaca: Cornell University Press.

Harding, Sandra. 1986. *The Science Question in Feminism,* Ithaca: Cornell University Press Healthcare Labour Adjustment Agency. 1996. *Bulletin,* 28 June, 2:3.

Health and Welfare Canada. 1985. *Privatization in the Canadian Health Care System: Assertions, Evidence, Ideology and Options,* Ottawa: Health and Welfare Canada.

Health Canada. 1998. *Shared Responsibilities: Shared Vision,* Ottawa: Health Canada.

Health Canada. 1999. *Health Reform Data Base Overview by Province, 1998-99,* Ottawa: Health Canada.

Himmelstein, David U. and Steffie Woolhandler. 1994. *The National Health Program Book,* Monroe, ME: Common Courage Press.

Jerome-Forget, Monique and Claude E. Forget. 1998. *Who Is The Master? A Blueprint for Canadian Health Care Reform,* Montreal: The Institute for Research on Public Policy.

Jönsson, Bengt. 1996. "Making Sense of Health Care Reform." In *Health Care Reform: The Will to Change.* Paris: OECD.

Jutras, Sylvie and Frances Veilleux. 1991. "Informal Caregiving: Correlates of Perceived Burden", *Canadian Journal on Aging,* 10(1): 45-55.

Kleiber, Nancy and Linda Light. 1978. *Caring for Ourselves: An Alternative Structure for Health Care,* Vancouver: BC Public Health.

Koivussalo, Meri and Eeva Ollila. 1997. *Making a Healthy World: Agencies, Actors & Policies.* In *International Health,* London: Zed Books.

Lawrence, Carmen. 1996. "Opening Statement." OECD.

Lesemann, Frederic. 1984. *Services and Circuses,* Montreal: Black Rose Books.

Lesemann, Frederic and Daphne Nahmiash. 1993. "Home-Based Care in Canada and Quebec." In Frederic Lesemann and Claude Martin (eds.), *Home-Based Care: The Elderly, the Family and the Welfare State: An International Comparison,* Ottawa: University of Ottawa Press.

Laurence, Leslie and Beth Weinhouse. 1997. *Outrageous Practices: How Gender Bias Threatens Women's Health,* New Brunswick: Rutgers University Press.

Maher, Janet. 1993. "Healthcare in Crisis." *Healthsharing,* 14(2):13.

Marmot, M.G., Rose G. Shipley, M.Hamilton. 1978. "Employment Grade and Coronary Heart Disease in British Civil Servants." *Journal of Epidemiology and Community Health* 32,:244-9.

Marsh, Leonard. 1975. *Report on Social Security for Canada 1943,* Toronto: University of Toronto Press.

Martin, Brendan. 1993. *In the Public Interest? Privatization and Public Sector Reform,* London: Zed Books.

Martin, Paul Finance Minister. 1995. Budget Speech, February 27.

Maynard, Alan. 1996. "United Kingdom." In Dorland and Davis.

McDonnell, Kathleen (ed.). 1986. *Adverse Effects: Women and the Pharmaceutical Industry,* Toronto: Women's Press.

McDonnell, Kathleen and Mariana Valverde. 1985. *The Health Sharing Book*, Toronto: Women's Press.

McIlroy, Ann.1999. "Canadians' Medical Data Should Be On Computer, Panel Says." *The Globe and Mail*, 4 February, p. A4.

McKenna, Barrie. 1996. "Provinces Take Steps to Shield Health Care." *The Globe and Mail*, March 26:B1.

McLeod, Linda. 1980. *Wife Battering in Canada: The Vicious Circle*, Ottawa: The Canadian Advisory Council on the Status of Women.

Mendelson, Michael. 1997. *The Capitalist Models: Where They Came from and Where They May Go*, Ottawa: Caledon Institute of Social Policy.

Megyery, Kathy and Frank Sader. 1996. *Facilitating Foreign Participation in Privatization*, Washington: the World Bank.

Mimoto. H and P. Cross. 1991. "The Growth of the Federal Debt." *The Canadian Economic Observer*, June, 1:1-17.

Mitchinson, Wendy. 1998. "Agency, Diversity, and Constraints: Women and Their Physicians, Canada 1850-1950." In Sherwin, Susan. "Introduction." In Susan Sherwin (coordinator), *The Politics of Women's Health: Exploring Agency and Autonomy*, Philadelphia: Temple University Press.

Moss, Kary L. 1996. *Man-Made Medicine: Women's Health, Public Policy and Reform*, Durham: Duke University Press.

Montreal Women's Press. 1968. *The Birth Control Handbook*, Montreal: Montreal Women's Press.

National Forum on Health. 1997. "Directions for a Pharmaceutical Policy in Canada." In *Canada Health Action: Building on the Legacy. Synthesis Reports and Issues Papers*. Ottawa: Minister of Public Works and Governmental Services.

National Forum on Health. 1997. *Health and Health Care Issues: Summaries of Papers commissioned by the National Forum on Health*. Ottawa: Minister of Public Works and Government Services Canada, February.

National Forum on Health. 1997. "Striking a Balance Working Group Synthesis Report." *Canada Health Action: Building on the Legacy.Volume ll. Synthesis Reports and Issues Papers*, Ottawa: Minister of Public Works and Government.

Naylor, David. 1986. *Public Payment, Private Practice*, Montreal: McGill-Queen's University Press.

Nelson, Joyce. 1995. "Dr. Rockefeller Will See You Now." *Canadian Forum*, January-February, 1995.

Neysmith, Sheila and Jane Aronson. 1996. "Home Care Workers Discuss Their Work: The Skills Required to 'Use Your Common Sense'." *Journal of Aging Studies*, 10(1):1-14.

Neysmith, Sheila and Jane Aronson. 1997. "Working Conditions in Home Care: Negotiating Race and Class Boundaries in Gendered Work." *International Journal of Health Services*, 27(3):479-99.

Oakley, Ann. 1990. "Who's Afraid of the Randomized Controlled Trial? Some Dilemmas of the Scientific Method and 'Good' Research Practice." In Helen Robert (ed.), *Women's Health Counts*, London: Routledge.

Organization for Economic Co-operation and Development. 1992. *The Reform of Health Care: A Comparative Analysis of Seven OECD Countries*, Paris: OECD.

Organization for Economic Cooperation and Development. 1995.*Governance in Transition: Public Management Reforms in OECD Countries*, Paris: OECD.

Organization for Economic Cooperation and Development. 1996. *Health Reform: The Will To Change*, Paris: OECD.

Organization for Economic Cooperation and Development. 1998. *The Future of Female Dominated Occupations*, Paris: OECD.

Osborne, David and Ted Gaebler. 1992. *Reinventing Government: How the Entrepreneurial Spirit is Transforming the Public Sector*, New York: Plume, 1992.

Overall, Christine. 1993. *Human Reproduction: Principles, Practices and Policies*, Toronto: Oxford.

Pacific Public Affairs Limited. 1993. *"New Directions": Anticipated Changes to the Regional Structure of the Health Care System.* Victoria: March:1, mimeo.

Panic, Mica. 1995. "The Bretton Woods System: Concept and Practice." In Jonathan Michie and John Grieve Smith (eds.). *The Global Economy*, Oxford: Oxford University Press.

Statistics Canada. 1997. *Earnings of Women and Men, 1995*, Ottawa: Minister of Industry, Table 2.

Paquet. Gilles and Robert Shepherd. 1996. "The Program Review Process: A Deconstruction." In Pederson, Ann, Michel O'Neill and Irving Rootman (eds.). 1994. "Preface." *Health Promotion in Canada: Provincial, National and International Perspectives.* Toronto: W.B. Saunders.

Petchesky, Rosalind Pollack. 1995. "From Population Control to Reproductive Rights: Feminist Fault Lines", *Reproductive Health Matters*, 6, November:152-161.

Peterson, Mark A. 1997. "Introduction: Health Care Into the Next Century", *Journal of Health Politics, Policy and the Law*, 22(2), April:291-313.

Pierre, Jon. 1995. "The Marketization of the State: Citizens, Consumers, and the Emergence of the Public Market." In B. Guy Peters and Donald J. Savoie (eds.), *Governance in a Changing Environment*, Montreal: McGill-Queen's University Press.

Rappolt, Susan G. 1997. "Clinical Guidelines and the Fate of Medical Autonomy in Ontario." *Social Science and Medicine,* 44(7):977-87.

Rehner, Jan. 1989. *Infertility: Old Myths, New Meanings*, Toronto: Second Story Press.

Rekart, Josephine. 1993. *Public Funds, Private Provision*, Vancouver, UBC Press.

Renaud, Marc. 1987. "Reform or Illusion? An Analysis of the Quebec State Intervention in Health." In David Coburn, Carl D'Arcy, George Torrance and Peter New (eds.). *Health and Canadian Society*, 2nd Edition, Markham: Fitzhenry and Whiteside.

Report of the Eastman Commission of Inquiry on the Pharmaceutical Industry. 1985. Ottawa: Supply and Services Canada.

Ruggie, Mary. 1996. *Realignments in the Welfare State: Health Policy in the United States, Britain, and Canada*, New York: Columbia University Press.

Ryten, Eva. 1997. *A Statistical Picture of the Past, Present and Future of Registered Nurses in Canada*, Ottawa: Canadian Nurses Association, Table 3.

Sainsbury, Diane. 1996. *Gender, Equality and Welfare States*, Cambridge: Cambridge University Press.

Scarpaci, Joseph (ed.). 1989. *Health Services Privatization in Industrial Societies*, New Brunswick: Rutgers University Press.

Schwartz, Bryan Dr. 1996. "NAFTA Reservations in the Areas of Health Care." Winnipeg, Manitoba. File No. 24703, March 4:1.

Shapiro, Evelyn. 1997. *The Cost of Privatization: A Case Study of Manitoba*, Ottawa: Canadian Centre for Policy Alternatives.

Sherwin, Susan. 1992. *No Longer Patient: Feminist Ethics and Health Care*, Philadelphia: Temple University Press.

Sherwin, Susan. 1998. "Introduction." In Susan Sherwin (coordinator), *The Politics of Women's Health: Exploring Agency and Autonomy*, Philadelphia: Temple University Press.

Shields, John and B. Mitchell Evans. 1998. *Shrinking the State: Globalization and Public Administration "Reform"*, Halifax: Fernwood.

Shortell, Stephen M., Robin R. Gillies, David A. Anderson, Karen Morgan Erickson and John B. Mitchell. 1996. *Remaking Health Care in America,* San Francisco: Jossey-Bass.

Simmons, Harvey.1990. *Unbalanced: Mental Health Policy in Ontario, 1930-1989*, Toronto: Wall and Thompson.

Sky, Laura. 1995. *Lean and Mean Health Care: The Creation of the Generic Worker and the Deregulation of Health Care*. Working Paper 95-3, Health Research Project, Ontario Federation of Labour, June.

Sparr, Pamela (ed.). 1994. *Mortgaging Women's Lives: Feminist Critiques of Structural Adjustment*, London: Zed.

Starr, Paul. 1987. *The Limits of Privatization*, Washington: Economic Policy Institute.

Statistics Canada. 1993. *91 Census, Industry and Class of Worker*, Ottawa: Minister of Industry, Science and Technology.

Stein, Jane. 1997. *Empowerment and Women's Health Theory, Methods and Practice,* London: Zed Books.

Stoddart, Greg, Morris Barer, Robert Evans and Vanda Bhatia. 1993. "Why Not User Charges? The Real Issues." Toronto: The Ontario Premier's Council on Health, Well-Being and Social Justice.

Struthers, James. 1997. "Reluctant Partners. State Regulation of Private Nursing Homes in Ontario, 1941 72." In Raymond B. Blake, Penny E. Bryden and J. Frank Strain (eds.). *The Welfare State in Canada: Past, Present and Future*, Toronto: Irwin.

Sutherland, Ralph and Jane Fulton. 1994. *Spending Smarter and Spending Less: Policies and Partnerships for Health Care in Canada*, Ottawa: Canadian Hospital Association Press.

Swimmer, Gene. 1996. "An Introduction to Life Under the Knife." In Gene Swimmer (ed.), *How Ottawa Spends: Life Under the Knife*, Ottawa: Carleton University Press.

Taylor, Malcolm. 1987. *Health Insurance and Canadian Public Policy*, 2nd edition. Montreal: McGill Queen's University Press.

The Toronto Star. 1999. "'Report Cards' Proposed for Health-Care Services", 4 February:A6.

Thorpe, Kenneth E. 1997. "The Health System in Transition: Care, Cost and Coverage", *Journal of Health Politics, Policy and the Law*, 22(2), April:339-361.

Walker, William. 1999. "PM Forging Ahead on Health Accord." *The Toronto Star*, 27 January, p. A7.

White, Jerry. 1990. *Hospital Strike: Women, Unions, and Public Sector Conflict*, Toronto: Thompson.

Wickens, Barbara. 1998."When Hospitals Lose Beds." *Maclean's,* June 15:21.

Working Group on Health Services Utilization. 1994. "When Less Is Better: Using Canada's Hospitals Efficiently." Conference of Federal/Provincial/Territorial Deputy Ministers of Health.

Working Group on Women and Health Reform. 1999. Health Canada.

World Health Organization. 1998. *The World Health Report 1998*, Geneva: World Health Organization.

Wotherspoon, Terry. 1990. "Immigration, Gender and Professional Labour: State Regulation of Nursing and Teaching." Paper presented to the CSAA 25th Annual Meeting, Victoria, B.C., May.

Wunderlich, Gooloo S., Frank A. Sloan and Carolyne K. Davis (eds.). 1996. *Nursing Staff in Hospitals and Nursing Homes: Is it Adequate?* Washington, DC.:National Academy Press.

AGMV
MARQUIS
Québec, Canada
2000